THE
FIRST
CRIME
SCENE

Lessons of Life Learned
at Crime Scenes of Death

By
Det. Frank Tomlinson, Ret.
LAPD Robbery Homicide Division

WGAw Registration 1298613
2828 Cochran Street #136
Simi Valley, CA 93065
(805) 558-2226

To my Beautiful daughter,
Thanx for teaching me about
story + editing.

2-12-10

1

ROBBERY HOMICIDE DIVISION 1974:   The commanding officer of the division, and the commanding officer of the Homicide Special Section, decide to break from the LAPD tradition of arbitrarily assigning partners. They take the unusual risk allowing two detectives of equal supervisory rank (D-3) to decide if they want to work with one another. If the risk fails, the C/O's would face department criticism for breaking with tradition.

This is the story of the experiment, and what it was like to chase killers a mere 35 years ago without DNA, computers, the internet, or cell phones. It is based on true events.

By all accounts, these were the glory years for LAPD.

INTRODUCTION

I've known Frank Tomlinson for decades. He joined the Los Angeles Police Department in 1961, two years prior to me. It was a time without the great advances of today. There was no DNA testing, no computers, no portable communication devices. Most importantly there was no body armor which would have stopped the bullet that penetrated Frank's back during a brawl with suspects, a brawl in which his partner was beaten into a coma.

Frank's stories are based on real cases, the tough murder investigations. He solved the cases the way the public and his colleagues expected them to be solved: Hard work, doggedness, seeing details by bits and pieces and putting them together to complete the puzzle, outstanding interview and interrogation techniques, toughness, and the ability to be cold, hard, or compassionate when necessary. He and his partner solved more cases than many other teams combined. They were given the freedom to pursue their investigations as they saw fit because they had the confidence of their bosses, and they produced results.

After 34 years on L.A.P.D. with various assignments and being involved in politics (not the Department kind), I think I have developed a good read on people. With Frank I see a top-notch, dedicated and smart detective that knew how to get what he went after time and again.

This story is one of many and I hope Frank gives us more in the future, sharing with us the way real police work was once done.

It has been my privilege to know one of the best we had, who gave L.A.P.D. a great reputation.

Captain George Aliano, Ret.
Commanding Officer, LAPD Foothill Division (post Rodney King)
Past President, Los Angeles Police Protective League

I. *WILDERNESS*

Then they said to Moses, "Is it because there were no graves in Egypt that you have taken us away to die in the wilderness?" (Exodus 14:11)

The prick of the needle was the worst part. Hannah glanced at her extended left arm and noticed how innocent and white her skin looked. Quickly, she looked away as the needle pressed against her inner arm. Her heart raced as she anticipated the moments to follow, always aware that the man who controlled the needle had overdosed his own brother. But her longing for the rush overpowered her fears, and she laid her head back on the pillows. Her boyfriend kept her in nice digs, she thought as she looked up at the high white ceiling in the bedroom. "It's a nice life living in the Hollywood hills with all the H we'll ever need."

Jaden found her vein and gently pressed on the syringe. He watched Hannah close her eyes. His eyes were at half-mast, making him look sleepy although he felt alert.

Hooked as she was, Hannah still couldn't bring herself to put a needle into her own body. Jaden enjoyed knowing she was dependent upon him for this. He had faced the reality that without the heroin, she would not be with him. She was far too beautiful to be seen with a man so plain as he, physically and personality-wise.

"Like a thousand orgasms," Hannah whispered as the heroin pumped through her body. Jaden smiled a sinister half-smile, "Enjoy, baby, this is what we live for and we'll never stop." For a moment he wondered if he was trying to convince himself. His truth reminded him that no one who hasn't tried this could ever know how spectacular the feeling is.

Jaden was only thinking good thoughts now. His anger over the night before faded along with the pain in his jaw. He had waited for Hannah to return from her tryst with the senator. That was the only way they ever referred to him: The Senator. He always called when he was in the area and Hannah was eagerly available for him. She serviced him at the 9000 building on the Sunset strip. She wasn't bashful about giving Jaden all the details. The sexual conquest of a United States senator was too significant to keep to herself. And the cash she brought home made it even nicer.

But this night, Jaden had been out late himself. And when he walked into the bedroom to awaken her for his own pleasures, he was ignorant of the wet, sticky blood that stained his slacks. When Hannah sat up and saw the blood stain on her silk sheets, she reacted by punching Jaden in the face with her fist.

• • • • •

About forty miles northwest, in a mere middle-class neighborhood, I was feeling my own pain. It was three days before payday, and I sat looking at unpaid and overdue bills. Financial pressure was unrelenting. No matter how hard I worked, I could never quite make it from payday to payday. I spent so much time in the Police Credit Union that I married one of the loan officers. When we could no longer afford housing in the city, I moved my family outside of Los Angeles. Our new residence was not even accessible by freeway, and Los Angeles traffic was the worst part of working there.

As it turned out, a short time after we moved grading began for a new freeway. Forced busing of public school students had caused an exodus of people fleeing Los Angeles to escape the court-imposed mandate. No matter what the rulers said, the peasants were not willing to torture their children by sending them to faraway and dangerous places for school. My new community was only a short distance outside the city and since it was in another county, folks could keep their kids in schools close to home.

Once the earth was leveled to a fairly smooth surface and long before concrete was poured, I had the best imaginable private drive to Los Angeles. No traffic, no congestion, no signals; I only had to watch for ditches and earth movers as I sped along the ribbon of dirt being graded into the ground.

Was I lucky or what? Falling into situations that seemed to take no skill on my part was something I usually took credit for, but lucky breaks threatened my illusion that I had life under control. I had learned early in life to give the appearance that I always knew what I was doing and that good things happened exactly the way I planned them. I was an illusionist, but I made it work for me. Others saw me as the obnoxious and arrogant person that I was.

Although the drive to work became better than tolerable, the long hours required of a homicide detective were still grueling. Many nights I would push my undercover black 1972 Oldsmobile, as fast as it would go to get to my house before I fell asleep from exhaustion. Windows down, radio cranked up to a country station, I heard songs about life, love, heartache, gunfighters, and even a coal miner's daughter, but I never heard a love song for homicide detectives.

When I arrived home, usually in the middle of the night, my lovely wife would appear out of the dark when I opened the door. Dressed in a nightgown, she had an angelic appearance that I looked forward to seeing as I stepped into the house. Besides that, she always smelled good.

● ● ● ● ●

I was feeling especially drained this September morning in 1974. I had spent the evening into the early morning hours on a deserted stretch of Mulholland Drive where I had been called because a body had been found buried near the side of the road. It was dusk when I arrived; the sun had moved below the mountains to the west, but it wasn't dark yet. The usual detective and patrol vehicles were parked near the crime scene. Just like my Oldsmobile, the detective cars were easily identified by anyone paying attention. Four doors with plain tires and wheels; and the government-issued license plates were a dead giveaway. They just weren't painted black and white like the patrol cars that I pulled up next to.

Despite the car, mine was the dream job for anyone who loved police work the way I did. My supervisors, a captain and a lieutenant were friends who trusted me. When I balked at being transferred to Robbery Homicide Division, I was told that it was for an assignment that no other detective enjoyed. The captain already knew of my work and said he was bringing me to RHD to stay in the field and solve murders. In order to carry out this assignment, he lifted the burden of making appearances at the office, something that would have added hours of drive time to my work-day. He warned me that this would ostracize me from the other detectives in the division, who rarely left the office to investigate cases. They saw their assignment at RHD in a more traditional way, where one dressed properly in a white shirt and tie and made all of the appropriate phone calls in order to complete all of the proper reports. Even though crimes were rarely solved, official reporting was dutifully completed and that was enough to cover everyone's collective ass.

The captain had recently been assigned to head up RHD and confided to me that some of the detectives working there were suspicious of him, assuming he had been sent there to clean up one of the most elite divisions in police work anywhere. He said that the RHD mentality was deeply entrenched in some of the veteran detectives who maintained the illusion that RHD detectives were superior to the hard working and overloaded divisional detectives. Few cases were being solved at the homicide table. Alcohol was too big a problem to hide for some of the veteran detectives.

"They will be doubly suspicious of you," he warned, "because I brought you here. So do your job, but watch your back. I only expect to see you in this office on paydays." With that, I was set free to work alone since none of the other RHD detectives would want to work with me. My assignments would be given to me by the lieutenant whom the captain had handpicked to head up the homicide section of RHD.

What the captain told me about my assignment seemed too good to be true. Not only was I being invited to play in the major leagues, I was being trusted to play a position that no one else was playing.

• • • • •

It was important for a detective from RHD to be present at most homicide scenes in the city, as there was always a possibility the case would be turned over, then or later, to RHD. I was told that once a case was assigned to me, I would be trusted to investigate it regardless of time or travel.

The only downside to the assignment was a political component to the way homicides were assigned. The city was divided into 17 divisions, each having a full complement of detectives to handle all of the crimes reported within their jurisdiction. That meant divisional detectives were the first responders to homicide or death scenes.

For that reason, it was important to me that I build a rapport with these men, many of whom were so suspicious of the elitist attitude of RHD detectives that they resented calling them or seeing them at crime scenes. Since I was not required to work from the RHD offices, it gave me time to spend in the divisions building relationships with the detectives and patrol officers who did real police work.

The captain's predictions proved correct, as I was ignored or criticized by the other RHD detectives whenever I showed up at Parker Center. Of course, it hadn't helped when I showed up at the office wearing a pink shirt and flowered tie. I hadn't realized the emphasis on white shirts only, and was instantly regarded as RHD's token gay.

• • • • •

As I arrived at the crime scene on Mulholland Drive, I saw the homicide detectives from West Valley Division. They greeted me by name as I approached them. I enjoyed that they treated me as a peer. Everyone was standing in the dirt, about thirty yards off the paved road at the crest of a canyon that exposed the San Fernando Valley far below.

As I walked toward the grave, I felt the wind whistling over the top of the hillside on the south side of the road as it picked up speed and blew down into the canyon below the grave. Although this empty, howling wasteland on the north side of the Santa Monica Mountains had the feeling of being far removed from civilization, it was anything but that. The Santa Monica Mountains are the only range that transverses a major metropolitan city in North America. These mountains are dotted with mountain lions, bobcats, mule deer, rock singers, movie stars, writers and dead bodies. But the road actually led to nearby residences, they just couldn't be seen from here.

I wondered if the people who selected this burial site had weighed the risks of being spotted by a passing motorist. Perhaps that was the reason the grave had been dug behind a large shrub that blocked a clear view from the road.

The ground was dry and concrete-like. It would take time, tools, and hard work to make a dent in this stuff. Typically, graves dug in this type of dirt are shallow because of the back-breaking work involved. Still, someone would be crazy to dig a grave here if the body was nearby. More likely, the killer dug the hole first and then brought the body. This might someday make a case for premeditation, since the hole may have been dug before the murder had even occurred. Note-taking began.

Patrol officers stood nearby looking at the grave. When I was near enough, I saw the head, left shoulder and arm of a man's body protruding from the dirt. The tattoo on his left arm caught my attention. It was a USMC bulldog.

The detectives took me aside, away from their supervisors, to ask me if I would consider taking this case as there were no clues for them to begin working with and their workload was already wearing them out. There was a high probability this crime would be very hard, if not impossible, to solve. In their vernacular, it looked like a "who-done-it." This fit the criteria for cases RHD was designed to take, as divisional detectives did not have a lot of time to spend on complicated cases. Their divisional assignment required them to handle many crimes other than homicides and also included processing arrestees brought in by patrol officers.

The detectives brought me up to speed. A man had been driving over nearby trails in an all-terrain vehicle, when he saw a small pack of dogs digging and fighting nearby. He threw some rocks to chase them off. When they wouldn't leave he went to see what they were fighting over. He saw that they were tearing at something in a hole they had dug. He took a stick and poked into the hole and when he realized he was looking at a man's head, he panicked and ran back to his ATV. One of LAPD's air units was passing overhead and saw him running. He signaled to them that he needed help, and they sent a patrol unit to investigate.

That was really all that was known. We would wait for the coroner to arrive and extricate the body from its temporary grave. Perhaps there would be a clue buried with the victim, some identity or an evident cause of death.

Unlike crime scenes in an enclosed area, where an exhaustive and meticulous search can be conducted for clues and evidence, this crime scene consisted of a hole in the ground at the edge of a steep canyon in the wilderness. Even though every precaution would be taken to preserve evidence, there was only so much that was going to be accomplished outside in the gathering darkness, especially with the wind swirling dust all around.

The coroner and crime lab arrived soon after I did. As pictures were taken, one of the young patrol officers was smart enough to volunteer to find the nearest donut shop and bring back some coffee. He reminded me of my early years as a patrol officer in Kansas City, Missouri. I thanked him as I pulled some bills out of my pocket and handed them to him. I remembered the first time I was called to a death scene in K.C. While I stood staring at the victim's blood running down the sidewalk, a cynical old detective walked up next to me and said, "Makes you wish you had some bread, doesn't it?" Humor, often in its most callous form, was made for self-protection at scenes that shocked the senses.

But donuts always made sense and somehow made me feel better. The patrol officer took my money and drove away. I found out later that he stopped around the first bend where he exited his black-and-white and puked his guts out.

After the photographer finished, we began to carefully remove the dirt around the body. Daylight was fading fast and we decided to remove the body and secure the location until daylight. As the coroner lifted the body from its temporary grave, we saw that the victim was wearing a white shirt jacket, checkered pink pants and white boots. Rigor mortis had already passed, indicating the victim had been dead for more than 24 hours. The coroner found a gaping wound to the back of the head that appeared to be the likely cause of death. The victim's clothes were covered with dried bloodstains.

The only clues for the evening were a billfold and a long handled axe buried beneath the body. The rules said the coroner had to retain possession of personal items found on the body, so we went through the contents of the billfold while the coroner was loading the body into his van. A California driver's license identified the victim as Max, a 38-year-old male Caucasian. His address was in West Hollywood, on the south side of the mountains range.

Since the case would remain with divisional detectives until a formal request was made by their supervisors for RHD to take it, the detectives released the body to the coroner for an autopsy the next morning. Once we had dusted off the donuts and coffee, there was no further need for me to remain. It was now well after midnight. The divisional detectives said they would do some preliminary records checking the next morning if I would attend the autopsy. They were confident the investigation would be handed over to me. I raced home to get some sleep. The morgue was located downtown near the RHD offices at Parker Center. It would be a long drive, very early the next morning.

I made it home, fell into bed and was asleep before my head hit the pillow. I often wondered if anybody enjoyed sleep more than I did. It was excruciatingly painful every time I tried to wake up.

On this occasion, I managed to ignore the alarm until one of our kids started pounding on the locked bedroom door. Even then, my wife had to shake me awake. I found it hard to believe that my family had been awakened by the alarm clock before I was. Once awake, I yelled at my son, "Who dat bammin on my door?" I had these same words yelled at me many times when working patrol.

Going into the city meant putting on a tie and preparing for a long drive. I was too tired to remember which one I hated more.

● ● ● ● ●

Walking to the police entrance at the rear of the morgue was not a pleasant experience. From outside, the smells of death were like a slap in the face, an odor so repulsive that it seemed to possess a life of its own. That ghastly smell then penetrated my nostrils and clothes with the stench of spoiled blood. I was never able to enter these doors without encountering the smell.

This morning, I hesitated for a moment and imagined the odor as a vicious watch dog trying to warn me away from entering this dark, monstrous place.

Pushing the queasiness aside, I walked through the doors to see corridors lined with gurneys containing bodies. I walked through the hall toward the autopsy rooms, looking at each body for Max. The rows of gurneys in the hallways presented a gallery of death, some bodies mutilated, some dismembered, and some appearing healthy enough to stand up and leave.

Max was already in an autopsy room where his body had been prepped for this last bit of surgery, one that he could never have imagined, performed by a medical examiner he was never going to meet.

To my surprise, the West Valley detectives were waiting for me and they weren't smiling. They told me their captain wanted to retain the case for a while to see if something might surface in a day or two that would allow them to take credit for solving the murder. He wanted to make sure that there were no clues that would allow RHD to solve the case and take the credit. These political decisions were disheartening for all of us. Good detectives knew that the more one played games in the early hours of a murder investigation, the more it hindered a successful prosecution should the crime be solved. We also knew that solving the crime and punishing the killer were our priorities, but not necessarily those of our promotion-driven superiors.

But we were soldiers in a chain of command and we followed orders, even if we questioned the competence of those who issued them.

I remained to observe the autopsy. Under the bright lights, it became apparent that Max's injuries were much worse than they had appeared in the muted light on Mulholland Drive. The flesh on the top of his head was missing, eaten away by the animals that uncovered his grave. What had appeared to be blunt force trauma to the back of the victim's head were actually three deep wounds through the skull, exposing what brain matter was left uneaten. There was also one deep incision to the cheek. Looking at Max's neck made me believe the cheek wound was accidentally inflicted. The killer had been targeting Max's neck.

There are wounds of murder and there are wounds of rage. It was apparent that the killer had tried to decapitate Max, chopping most of the way through his neck.

The message of these wounds led me to believe that Max had been caught from behind by the axe that we found buried with him. The medical examiner had the axe and concluded that it was consistent with the wounds. The axe head was covered with blood that would be analyzed for blood type.

The fact that the suspect had not taken Max's identity made us wonder if the killer actually intended for the body to be found, mutilated as it was, in order to send a message to others.

There were many things to remember, clues to sort out regarding the suspect. Was he a badass or just a weak man who found digging a grave in hard ground too much work? I eliminated the likelihood of a female because of the physical strength it would take to move the body and dig the grave. I was leaning toward the theory of a physically weak killer because of the wounds delivered to the back of the head. I made a note to myself, "The killer may have sneaked up on the victim because he was too weak or too afraid to face him."

I should be able to find out if Max was himself a badass, and the Marine Corp tattoo told me that he might have been.

The rest of the examination was routine. The torso was opened and examined and organ samples taken. Food in the stomach indicated Max had eaten a short time before being killed. There were no needle marks, although we would wait for the results of toxicology tests to be certain about drug use. The medical examiner agreed with our opinion that our victim had been dead only two or three days.

• • • • •

Since I was wearing a tie, I stopped by RHD, arriving just before lunch. I thought it might help my image to be seen suited up and in a white shirt, like the other detectives. I would check in with the lieutenant, get something to eat at the police academy, stop by West Valley Station, then head home for more sleep.

I had one exceptionally good friend at RHD whom I always looked forward to seeing. Art was a story teller, so entertaining that no one could resist. To add to his stories, Art had a tic that caused him to keep looking over his shoulder as he talked, as if he was waiting for a character in his story to walk up behind him.

Art had been a member of the first Olympic basketball team, the one that began a dynasty for the USA in the 1936 Munich games. I hung out with him at golf courses, race tracks and poker games. I saw his pictures, awards and gold medal. He was a friend I respected and trusted.

Art had been recruited in the 1940's by LAPD to play on the department basketball team. The LAPD played against top notch college and AAU competition before the NBA was formed. The department realized having competitive sports teams was a good recruiting tool. He was also good friends with the captain who had been an All-American basketball player in college. Art would brag that he was the only policeman on the job to have never worked a day in a police uniform. Because of his basketball talent, he was assigned to vice upon leaving the academy, the better to be available for basketball gigs.

Art was in the middle of a story when I walked into RHD. When he saw me, he waved and quickly ended his story. He wanted me to go to lunch with him so we could try to get a pick-up basketball game at the academy. I was really tired, but I agreed. Art was about 25 years my senior, but he always surprised the competition with his energy and we dusted some young studs in a two-on-two half-court game. He and I frequently teamed up with the captain and visited open gyms just to surprise the young guys by being almost unbeatable in three-on-three games. It was fun to watch our competition get frustrated because they couldn't beat guys old enough to be their dads. Of course, they never knew the caliber of talent of the two guys I was playing with.

After showering and dressing, Art and I had hamburgers in the academy café. The urban legend was that Marilyn Monroe had worked here upon her arrival in Los Angeles and had dated a policeman whom she married. That didn't stop every policeman from fantasizing that had he been the one, it would have changed her life for the better.

By the time I got to West Valley, I was really dragging. I was actually pleased to discover that the homicide detectives were in the field and not available. I contacted them on the radio and arranged a meeting for the next morning. Then I hauled myself home for some sleep.

II. *JOHN DOE*

There is a way which seems right to a man, but its end is the way of death. *(Proverbs 14:12)*

Reaching home was bittersweet. I loved it, but felt bad because I had no energy to give to my wife or children. I typically ran so many hours of work together that when I walked through the door, I barely made it into the living room. My wife was always worrying about my health and one time had to help me get to the sofa when I stepped through the door and collapsed. I was putting in so many hours; I was ignoring the evidence that I had contracted walking pneumonia.

To make marriage and family more difficult, my wife wanted to know what I had been doing at work. That was impossible for me to answer. She would not be able to handle the brutality of my work, but when I made up some superficial answer, she became obsessed with the idea that I was hiding things from her like having another woman on the side. I saw many police marriages fail over this tension.

The need for policemen to unload the horrors of their job, often results in "choir practice" after their shift ends. They meet with other police and emergency room nurses at cop bars where they can drink and swap war stories. They feel these are the only people who can really understand them. They drift away from friends and acquaintances that do not live in their world of violence and misery. Their wives are not allowed to see this world; wives and children must be protected from it. The only other outsiders allowed in, are prostitutes. Nurses and prostitutes know something about the dark side of life.

I wished my wife could know, but I realized she did not have the capacity to comprehend my work and to tell her would only frighten her beyond what she could bear. In that respect, I was closer to some policemen, like Art, than I was to my wife.

● ● ● ● ●

The morning after Max's autopsy, my oldest son reminded me that it was Saturday, the day of his first Boy's Baseball team practice. I had forgotten. I called West Valley detectives and left a message that I would meet them later in the day so that I could watch my son play ball.

The weather was perfect for baseball, sunny and mid-80's. Although still tired, I played with the kids before we all headed to the practice field after breakfast. I followed my wife in my police car so that I could leave directly from the ballpark. I parked just beyond the left field fence. The coach sent my son to left field and, as I watched him, I became well aware of how little time I had spent helping him know how to play baseball. I felt ashamed as I saw him trying to follow the coach's instructions. He looked insecure, and I knew I had failed him. He was trying to figure out where the coach wanted him to stand and looked over his shoulder at me, as if he was embarrassed and afraid. I watched from my car as the coach shouted at him to stand just beyond the infield.

Suddenly, the police radio in my car blurted my call letters, "4K12." This was my office trying to contact me. I was told that officers were standing by at a crime scene just off the Hollywood freeway near downtown Los Angeles. They were waiting for me.

I rogered the call and looked at my son, wondering how I was going to tell him I had to leave for work. Just then, the coach hit a line drive toward left field. My son held up his gloved left hand to catch the ball, but it caught the tip of his finger instead of the pocket of the glove. The ball ripped the glove off his hand, and my son doubled over in pain, falling to his knees. He turned toward me with tears flowing down his cheeks, just in time to see me waving goodbye.

My wife called me later in the day to report that his finger was broken. My son never played baseball again. I will live the rest of my days remembering the look on the face of a ten-year-old boy longing for his dad to be there for him and with him.

The drive downtown was sobering. I wondered how a man is supposed to fulfill his responsibility to provide for his family, while giving each family member enough time to know how important they are to him. It seemed impossible to meet the demands of the job and the demands of a wife and children. It briefly entered my mind that maybe I should find another assignment, but I quickly suppressed the thought. I enjoyed my work far too much to give it up for anyone or anything. My next thought was that the work I did, and what the military did, should only be done by a single man, but it was too late for that. Then I remembered all the married men I knew in my work who were becoming single and it didn't help them become any better at work. So I consoled myself by cranking up the country station, feeling sorry for myself that nobody sings love songs for homicide detectives, or for their children who feel orphaned, or for their wives who feel widowed.

• • • • •

When I arrived at the crime scene, I met the homicide detectives from Rampart Division. They had already determined that they would keep this case, but asked me to attend the autopsy the next morning. Bob, the officer in charge of Rampart detectives was a friend of mine and I agreed to help them. I had no way of knowing who was too busy to attend autopsies and who just didn't want to go through the ugly experience. Some detectives would find any excuse to avoid going. I knew detectives in both camps and reminded myself to discuss it with Bob at our next poker party.

The body was lying in the ivy just off the shoulder of the freeway. It had been discovered by a Caltrans worker who had called the police. I looked over the scene and made some notes in the event the case ever ended up with me. As far as we could see, the victim had suffered a single gunshot wound to the abdomen. He was a nicely dressed white guy in business clothes, and since there was no vehicle in sight, it was anybody's guess as to how or why he had been left at this location. No identification was found on his body.

I completed my notes at the crime scene and went to West Valley to see what progress the detectives there had made with Max's murder. They told me that the night before they had met a woman named Krissy when they went to the address on Max's driver's license. They got the impression that Krissy was a hooker who worked the nearby Sunset Strip. She was appropriately distraught over the news that Max's body had been found; their word for her was "shattered." They felt they had established some rapport with her but said she was clearly frightened and it would take some time to convince her to cooperate.

Then they laid the news on me that drove homicide detectives insane: since they had not made enough progress to satisfy their captain, and since they had other work that was backing up, their captain decided to transfer the case to RHD after all. This meant that an already gun-shy witness was now going to be contacted by a different detective to go over the same ground that she had already covered. If she was uncertain about talking to the police before, this would not give her a lot of confidence that the police knew what they were doing. Situations like this made it clear to us that the police command didn't know what the hell they were doing.

• • • • •

I was relieved when I called Krissy and she agreed to see me that evening. Since I had Krissy's phone number, I paid a visit to a woman who was brilliant at getting information from the phone companies. She ran a small PI office near the police academy and we had met by chance. She enjoyed hearing about the cases I was working on and seemed to take pleasure whenever she could help me, never asking for money or favors in return. I asked if she could find out the business information on the phone number Krissy was using. My friend made a call and said the phone was installed for Patricia Haze at the address on Max's driver's license.

I arrived at Krissy's after dark. She invited me in and introduced me to a girlfriend of hers who was obviously there for protection in case my visit didn't go well. I assumed the other woman was Patricia Haze, but Krissy introduced her as Pam.

Krissy lived on second floor of a nice apartment building. Her front door opened directly into a large living room that was clean and nicely furnished. The women mixed drinks in the kitchen and offered me one. Although I wasn't a drinker I decided to accept, hoping to break the ice. It seemed to work.

Krissy lived alone. She worked the Strip, which was only a couple of blocks from her apartment. She and Max often went to the clubs together. She had met him some years earlier when she was living in Alaska and he was performing at clubs up there. Krissy was immediately attracted to him because he was sensitive and funny. They moved in together, and she saw that he was actually dark and troubled. He had his own band. He played drums and was the lead singer. He dreamed of opening his own club.

When Max's closest friend in the band overdosed on heroin and died, he took it hard and left Alaska. He had been out of her life for a number of years, and suddenly showed up again a few months ago.

After about an hour, Krissy said she was tired and asked me and Pam into the bedroom to continue. Her bed was a California king with a canopy. It was covered with a pink silk comforter and many pillows. Krissy lay across the bed while Pam sat in an armchair nearby. I felt Krissy was beginning to sense that I was safe enough to talk to, so I sat on the corner of the dresser and pressed her a bit for more detailed information.

She had last seen Max on Friday a week ago. He left her apartment in the early evening to meet with friends at the Rainbow Club on Sunset Boulevard. He said he had business to take care of and that it would be better if she didn't go.

Before leaving, he shocked her by asking her to marry him. She rolled onto her back, staring at the canopy as if she was answering

Max again as she repeated what she told him, "I love you. Will you give me some time to think about it?"

Krissy turned back toward me and I could see tears in her eyes. "He said he would give me two days and he'd come back on Sunday for my answer." She said she never saw him again. He had not told her where he was staying, so she had no way to contact him.

Krissy said the friends Max was leaving to meet were Barry, Jaden and Luis. When Max did not return on Sunday, she checked the clubs and also called her friends. He had been seen with Luis Friday night, but no one had seen either of them after Friday night.

She continued, "Max talked about taking a once-in-a-lifetime chance at doing a really big dope deal. I never knew him to use hard drugs, but he tried to convince me that he could make enough money to finance his dream. He wanted to open his club in Hawaii. He had been there with the Marines. That was to be a new start for us to begin our married life."

The tears were flowing now. "I was going to tell him that I would marry him. I was madly in love with him. I'll never get to tell him now."

The more Krissy talked, the more she revealed information that could put her at risk. "Jaden and Luis are major dealers. Barry is one of their mules. Jaden is from the East Coast. He lives in a big hillside home above the Strip with a top-dollar hooker named Hannah. Hannah lived with me for a while before moving in with Jaden. She was using the name Patricia Haze and skipped out on the rent when she moved in with Jaden. Luis is from Colombia and lives near the Strip, closer to Hollywood. Jaden deals heroin and Luis cocaine. Barry has been in and out of prison and is a hustler who'll do anything for money."

She pulled an address book from a night stand and provided me the address and phone number for Jaden and Hannah. She had no contact information for Barry and wondered aloud if Max might have been staying with him.

I asked about her remark that Max was troubled. She said when he first showed up a couple of months ago, he was different. "He had his hair in an afro and was talking jive, like he was taking on a black personality. He dressed like a soul brother, flashy clothes and floppy brimmed hats. I had never seen him act like this before. That was the first time he began talking about pulling off a big dope deal."

Krissy paused and asked me if I'd like another drink. I declined, but she went into the kitchen to fix herself another. After she returned to the bed, she continued. "He tried to pull off a deal and got busted. He called me right after he bailed out of jail. He said Barry was busted with him and he thought Barry must have snitched him off. I didn't question him. I knew he had gotten close to Jaden. He started crying when I asked him what he had gotten himself into."

● ● ● ● ● ●

Krissy continued, "Max told me when he returned to L.A., he met a guy in Malibu who said he knew some guys who were looking to buy multi-pounds of heroin. He said he had seen Jaden handle really big deals, up to 100 kilos, so he told this guy that he had the connection the guy was looking for.

"He told me that Jaden made him feel like shit when he offered the deal to him. He said it was obvious that Jaden didn't want to cut him in on anything big. He said he figured a way to get around Jaden.

"Jaden told him that one of his muscle guys, a big black dude named Carl, would check out Max's information. Jaden told him that Carl and his friends worked as bouncers for Earl, a nightclub owner in Hollywood. He stalled Jaden by telling him he'd get back to him with more information. He wasn't about to give Jaden his new connection in Malibu."

22

I interrupted to ask Krissy who Earl was. She seemed surprised. "He tells everybody he pays off LAPD to leave him alone. He says that's why he never gets busted. He owns clubs in Hollywood, and everybody knows he sells drugs. He's really big in gay porn and a lot of porn stars hang out in his clubs. You know, people like John Holmes. You've seen the Johnny Wadd flicks, right?"

I didn't tell her I had never heard of Holmes or Wadd as I didn't want to appear uncool. However, I felt compelled to defend my department by telling her, "Then his bullshit story works." Krissy asked me what I meant and I explained, "Earl wants people to think he's got connections with the police. It works for intimidation."

Krissy looked puzzled by my remarks, but continued telling me about Max. "He told me he had the guy in Malibu go ahead and set up the deal to go down at the IHOP by the pier in Santa Monica. There were three guys making the buy. Max asked Barry to help by meeting the buyers at the Malibu connection's house. I asked for the name of this dope dealer in Malibu and Krissy said she only heard Max refer to him as George.

"Max said he had been fronted five kilos of heroin, but he didn't tell me where he got it. Max only took one kilo to the deal, so he could see if the buyers passed the test.

"If the deal went down smooth, the buyers told Barry they would take the other four kilos. The first kilo was sold for $30,000. The buyers showed up and handed Barry a briefcase with the cash. Barry went to the trash bins behind the IHOP where he opened the case and counted the cash. Then Max and Carl took the heroin out of Carl's VW and delivered it to the buyers to be tested."

Max told me he made a mistake by flashing a gun. "Carl and I were packing. When the buyers saw my gun they identified themselves as DEA and told us we were under arrest. Carl made a

23

run for it, but there were other agents in the parking lot and they caught him."

Max was paranoid because he had talked Carl into going along as his muscle without telling Jaden. He said he panicked while he was in jail and decided to call Jaden. He thought it would be better if he told him instead of waiting for Carl to do it. He tried to take the heat off Carl by telling Jaden that Barry had set everything up, and that Max and Carl thought he had told Jaden what they were doing. He then tried to lay everything off on Barry by saying he must be a snitch.

Max said Jaden went crazy. He knew that Jaden's connected to organized crime in Detroit where he transports heroin from Mexico, and that he knows plenty of guys who would make a hit for him.
Max told me he was just going to kill himself rather than wait for Jaden to have him tortured to death. Krissy was sobbing now. She stopped long enough to get some tissues and blow her nose.

"I begged him to tell me where he was so I could come and get him. He said he was making bail and then was going to Malibu. Jaden was separated from his wife, who lived in Malibu, so I figured Max might go to her for help. She might have been putting up his bail as Jaden owns a house there. I drove to a place on the beach where he liked to go and found him sprawled out in the sand. I brought him home and took care of him. He told me he'd swallowed a bottle of prescription pills that he stole from Jaden's wife."

Krissy wanted to keep talking, but it was already after midnight and I had another early morning autopsy to attend. I warned Krissy and Pam to be extremely careful not to tell anyone about my visit. I got Pam's contact information. Working girls have a tendency to think they can handle anything, so to emphasize my concern I told Krissy that I wanted a list of all of her regular johns in case she disappeared. I was hoping she was going to be my eyes and ears on the street for a while.

She told me Jaden was planning a huge Hollywood party at his place for the coming weekend. She said there would be lots of celebrities and drugs, but that no one could get in that Jaden did not know or invite. She had been invited by Luis.

● ● ● ● ● ●

I played back Krissy's story in my head on the long drive home. Thinking about Earl caused my mind to wander to an incident that had brought me to Los Angeles. When I told my dad I was applying for a job with the Kansas City, Missouri PD, he got angry. "The department's corrupt," he said, "and I don't want you working there. I'll get you into the union with me."

After I became a policeman, I was cruising alleys in downtown Kansas City, when I happened upon a new Cadillac blocking an alley. It was parked adjacent to a nightclub. No one was in the car, but a large man in a suit was standing at the entrance to the club. I asked him nicely if he knew when the car would be moved. He said, "That's none of your business." I went to my patrol car and took out my ticket book. The man came over and knocked it out of my hands, telling me if I knew what was good for me I'd drive away. He made the mistake of turning to walk away, exposing himself to a choke hold. Because I was taller than he, I was able to pull him backward and he was unconscious in about 20 seconds. I was still a rookie and forgot that it was not good to release an unconscious person face down. When I did, the man's face hit the pavement hard enough to bounce and I saw blood starting to run from beneath his head. I handcuffed him and pulled him into the police car, took him to headquarters and booked him for assaulting a policeman.

When I reported for duty the next night, my watch commander, Sgt. Kelly, took me aside. "You know I like you, Duke, but there are some things you have to learn. I can't tell you why, but that club where you made the arrest is off limits to us. The guy you booked was released before you got home last night. He's really pissed because you busted up his face, and his connections have already let the chief know. These are guys you don't want to mess with so I'm telling you, if you've ever thought of moving to another city, I would go there as soon as possible and it should be far away."

My dad hadn't told me the whole story. As a heavy gambler indebted to local bookies, and as a union man who had seen mobsters hospitalize workers who didn't vote Democrat, he knew Kansas City was run by the Syndicate. The club where I had made the arrest belonged to them. I was soon on my way to apply for a job with the LAPD.

● ● ● ● ● ●

The next morning, I was the sleepy guy in the suit. It was after a weekend of mayhem in Los Angeles, and the morgue was stacked up with the bodies of new visitors. As I walked down the hallway toward the autopsy room, I looked at each body, wondering what they would have done differently had they known they'd be spending their weekend at the morgue.

I was looking for the body of the man I had seen the day before next to the freeway. I found him in the wash room. He looked so different that it caught me off guard. In preparation for his autopsy, his clothes had been removed and his body had been scrubbed clean. He had been placed on his side and appeared to be looking for me as I walked in. I was taken aback at how he looked like me. He was the same age, the same size, 6'4" and 220 pounds. He had the same build and his hair was receding just like mine.

His face was unmarked; it appeared as if he had shaven shortly before he was killed. The small entry wound on his abdomen could hardly be seen, and he looked healthy enough to sit up and talk to me.

I had learned to get through autopsies by viewing the repulsive process the same way I would examine any piece of evidence, in other words by not making it personal. But this was different; this was surreal and personal in a way that I couldn't shake. I was uncomfortably aware that on any given day, I could be lying on one of these cold gurneys and some dumb detective could be staring at me, wondering what my last moments of life were like.

Without any plan on my part, my thoughts went to God. I had always believed that there was a God and that I was one of the good guys that He liked. As I watched this victim being dissected, I wondered about the basis for my beliefs. Even though I told myself I believed in God, I had absolutely no idea who He was or why people like this man died a violent death at such an early age. When I walked away from the shell of a body left on the gurney, I was shaken by the finality of it all. None of the dead people in this place was going to have a second chance to decide what they believed.

● ● ● ● ● ●

I made a conscious decision to conduct an investigation of my own beliefs. I had always resisted Christianity because of the Christians that I had met or seen on television. Raised in the Roman Catholic Church, I had become disillusioned by the repetitive predictability of the mass which never changed anything for me or my Catholic friends, so I just stayed away from anything religious.

My mother had told me that when I was born the doctor didn't know if either of us was going to make it. I have the receipt from the hospital. My mother and I were kept for a week before being discharged. The total bill was $28.50. My mother had written on her admittance forms that she was a Roman Catholic, so a Catholic priest was called to give us last rites. He asked my dad if he was a Catholic and when my dad said he was not, the priest turned to my mother and told her God was punishing her for being married to a heathen. He started to tell her that she had to divorce my dad in order for God to heal her, but my dad physically threw him out of the room before he could finish. Mocking Christians as weak fools became one way that I could briefly get on my dad's good side. As I thought all of this through, I remembered what my dad had taught me about being a real man. "Never show any weakness," he often repeated to me, and he lived this out in everything I saw him do. I had always seen Christians as weak and naïve, the kind of people I would never want to be identified with.

● ● ● ● ● ●

With the completion of the autopsy, a toe tag was placed on the victim, coldly identifying him as John Doe. My notes from the crime scene were borne out. A single shot from a .22 caliber handgun had been the cause of death. Because of the small caliber, the bullet didn't have enough fire-power to exit the victim's body. If Mr. Doe had been shot with a bigger gun, it would have passed through his body without striking any organs and would not have been fatal. But the small .22 bullet, on the way out of his body, had struck the backside of his ribcage and ricocheted into his heart. As the medical examiner finished his notes, he said, "Poor fellow, he probably would have thought he was lucky to be shot with a .22 instead of a bigger gun. Wonder what he thought he was going to be doing today?"

His organs had been removed and weighed, samples taken and the rest bagged up. As the ME dumped the mess back into the man's chest cavity, a squad of officers-in-training from the police academy slithered into the autopsy room from the hallway. The Rampart detectives and I lingered a bit longer to watch, remembering the shock of watching our first autopsy. The squad was herded around a gurney containing the corpse of a male and urged by the ME to move close. They were trying to act as if it didn't bother them, but the pale faces and body language revealed they wanted to be somewhere else. Just as the ME had done at my first autopsy, he removed a saw and made the first incision, which is to cut through the skull from ear to ear across the crown of the head. He then smiled and paused, carefully putting the saw down. His next move was deliberately in slow motion. He wedged his fingers into the edge of the incision at the top of the head and pulled the man's skin forward and down, so that his skin was covering his face. "Can any of you tell me why I do this first?" he asked the recruits. In the silence, he answered his question, "Because I don't want him to see what I'm going to do next." That crypt humor again. The recruits chuckled because it was still too horrible being here to laugh. But the Rampart detectives were roaring and the recruits knew they were being mocked. So as the ME took a scalpel and made a "Y" incision on the man's torso, I reached my hand into some running water and flicked it on the back of the head of one of the detectives. Wow, did he jump. He even startled me, and now the recruits were laughing out loud.

As I left the building, one of the coroner's investigators let me know that he was following up some leads about the victim's identity. He asked me if I wanted him to call me or Rampart detectives. I asked him to do both.

Since I was suited up, I stopped at the RHD office. The captain and lieutenant had received the request to take Max's case and asked for my opinion. After complaining once more about the way the LAPD allowed cases to be bounced around, I filled them in on my meeting with Krissy and the party that Jaden was throwing that evening. I told them I wanted to try to interview Jaden before his party. Out of concern for my safety, I was asked to take one of the other detectives with me. Art was playing golf, so a detective named Matt from the robbery team was asked to accompany me. I had played basketball with Matt and knew him to be a nice guy. We just worked different specialties.

I also knew there was a guy on the robbery team whom I had met before and was very impressed with. His name was Sammy, and to keep me humble, the captain told me that I wasn't the first person he brought to RHD, Sammy was. I had asked Sammy if he would partner up with me, but he said he already told the robbery team he would stay with them. I asked Rock if Sammy could work with me on my interview of Jaden and he said the robbery lieutenant had specifically asked him to keep me away from Sammy. He didn't want Sammy to get any ideas about changing assignments.

In planning the interview, I tried to think of what Jaden might expect me to do, so that I could do or say something that would surprise him. It was my experience that if I could confuse a suspect, he or she would be caught off-guard and make a mistake.

Since Matt had never worked with me, he assumed we would do everything by the book.

I used the number Krissy had given me to contact Jaden. When he answered, it was another confirmation of her credibility as a witness. It was Jaden's number and he sounded nervous when I asked for a meeting to discuss a murder case. It was strange that he didn't ask me who had been killed, only that he was leaving town and would be unavailable for an unknown period of time. When I told him I was only a few minutes away and coming to his house, he said he could meet, but only briefly.

I hung up the phone and saw Matt with a brief case used for recording interviews. I explained to him that I had never recorded a first interview with anyone, but he was concerned and said he'd feel better if we followed the book. Watching him try to set up the recorder, I realized he had never used this device before. He asked several of the robbery detectives before finding one who showed him how to work the thing. The trigger to switch the recorder on was located under the briefcase handle. He was told to place a legal pad inside the briefcase, over the recorder so that when he opened the briefcase he could remove the tablet, giving the suspect the impression that it was nothing more than a briefcase. He was also advised to practice using the recorder before he tried it on an interview. While I briefed the lieutenant on my plan, I saw Matt speaking into the briefcase, recording his voice and then playing it back until he was satisfied that he knew how to use it.

LAPD had no police station in West Hollywood. It was county territory and I had been using the West Hollywood sheriff's station as an office when working in the area. I had gotten to know some of the detectives there, and they were interested in the cases I was working. I drove Matt to the sheriff's station in order to advise the detectives of our plan. Jaden's home was in their jurisdiction. They introduced me to one of their narcotics officers. I discovered that he knew Luis and he confirmed that Luis was a major player in cocaine trafficking. He did not know Jaden. I told him about the party Jaden was planning, hoping he could get an informant or one of their undercover officers inside.

III. *JADEN*

What the wicked fears will come upon him. (Proverbs 10:24)

Matt and I set out from the West Hollywood sheriff's station into the estates in the hills north of the Sunset strip. Hannah answered the door of the plush hillside home. There was no mistaking why her services rated top dollar. She was tall, shapely and beautiful with long blonde hair and soft blue eyes. She appeared nervous as she invited us inside.

The furnishings were expensive but not gaudy. In fact, the house had the feel of being empty, and I assumed furniture had already been moved for the upcoming party. Our footsteps echoed around us as we walked through the entry and living room. I casually looked around for damage or blood that could have been left from an altercation. Killing Max was a bloody mess wherever it was done. Nothing appeared to be out of the ordinary.

Jaden was waiting in an area off the living room. The area was simply furnished with a colorful easy chair and a large white sofa. A coffee table of dark wood with a glass top was arranged between. There were paintings on the wall, but beside those and a table lamp on a side table, nothing else was in the room.

Jaden had a frail appearance with a soft handshake, fitting my image of a weak man. Immediately, I was suspicious. He was tentative as he directed us to sit on the sofa. He was nicely dressed in casual clothes and looked to be around thirty-five years old. His eyes were rat-like, small and busy, darting around first at Matt and then settling on me. Since Matt's intention was to record the conversation, he sat himself in front of the coffee table. He placed the briefcase on the table while I sat down next to him. Jaden's girlfriend slipped out of sight and Jaden sat down across from us, staring at me in silence. He was careful not to chance idle talk and waited for one of us to initiate the conversation. I waited for Matt to get set-up with his toy and stared back at Jaden to see what he would do with silence. He had a hard time maintaining eye contact.

Matt finally popped open the briefcase lid and removed his yellow legal pad and a pen which he dutifully placed on the table. It was hard not to smile knowing how hard he had practiced this act. He was trying to play it cool. He closed the lid, and I watched his finger stealthily slide under the handle to the switch that activated the recorder.

Suddenly, with a blast that surprised all three of us, the silence was shattered with a blaring recording of Matt's voice bouncing off the walls, "Testing, testing, testing, this is Matt, this is Matt testing." Matt panicked and grabbed for the switch, knocking the briefcase onto the floor. Yes, Matt had forgotten to switch the recorder from "play" to "record" on his last practice run. This was too funny not to laugh, but I was laughing alone.

Matt managed to turn off the recorder. He put the briefcase back on the coffee table and sheepishly asked Jaden, "Shall we get started?" He retrieved his tablet and pen as if nothing had happened and this caused me to chuckle at how he posed with his pen.

Jaden's rat-eyes were bugging out and I could see his heart beating in his neck. He wanted to run, but seemed frozen for a moment. He had seen the cheese and was not getting close to the trap. After an awkward silence, he stood and walked away without speaking.

I called after him, "Jaden, if you won't talk to us we will have to talk to all of your acquaintances to get the answers to our questions. They might get the impression that you're a killer and an asshole. It won't be my fault." Actually, it would be, but I wanted him to think about it. He just kept walking.

Hannah appeared out of nowhere to rush us toward the front door. Matt's face was so red that it matched his power tie. I had worn a sports coat and Levis, but no tie. As I took a better look at Hannah, I noticed she appeared more sedated than nervous. On our way out, I stopped at the door and looked hard into her eyes. I stared for a moment wondering if she might be a weak link to Jaden. I wanted her to be thinking about when and where she would see me again. She was having difficulty focusing her eyes, her pupils were constricted.

On the way back to the station, I tried to encourage Matt by telling him things had worked out just fine and that he was a fun guy to work with. Jaden likely was not going to forget us now. It was not likely he would tell us anything anyway, and I liked the idea of making him paranoid. I told Matt I would continue to work with him when the occasion warranted, but that I didn't have a plan and was taking the rest of the weekend off. I suggested he take the briefcase home and let his kids teach him how to use it. He finally laughed.

What I didn't tell Matt or anyone else was that the image of John Doe was haunting me to the point that I promised myself I would get my hands on a Bible and start reading. I didn't know what I would find, but I had resolved that I couldn't straddle the fence on a matter that suddenly seemed of crucial importance. I could not live in denial of my mortality when death was not just a theory for me, but something I saw face-to-face on more days than not.

The rest of that Saturday I did not receive any calls from work. My wife's memory is that I never had a weekend off, nor did we go anywhere that I wasn't called back to work. I had planned to start reading, but couldn't find a Bible in the house, so I went to a local book store. I scanned through several versions to make sure I could understand the wording since the only Bible I remembered opening before was a King James Version and I could make no sense of the language.

Since I had not been churched, I started at the beginning of the book. It never occurred to me to open any book in the middle to read a couple of lines and try to figure out what it was about. I had no expectations as to what was going to happen, but I did know something about investigations. I wanted to investigate what the Bible had to say about God and about me.

That first reading captivated me with the story of the Garden of Eden and what happened immediately thereafter. I got through the first four chapters in Genesis and then put it aside to think about it. I had a sense that I would spend many hours pondering the beginning of the story. There was something really important in considering the environment where God intended us to live. One thing was clear; I was living far from the place that God described.

• • • • •

I received a call the next morning from Detective Headquarters. All of my witnesses and informants knew they could reach me anytime by calling DHQ who forwarded messages to my home phone. My business cards carried the phone number for RHD, but since I was seldom there it also had the number of DHQ where calls were answered 24/7.

I was told that Krissy had called in the early morning hours looking for me. She left a number that I recognized as the number for the West Hollywood detectives. When I called, none of the detectives knew about the call, so I waited until evening to talk to the detectives who knew me.
I was told that a group of people from a party in the hills had been brought to the station after midnight. Krissy was one of them. She had been questioned and released, but must have used one of their phones to try to contact me.

I reached Krissy at her home phone. She told me that Jaden's party had started out as everything he was hoping for. In his typical arrogant manner, he was showing off in front of his guests. She thought there were a couple of hundred people present. He had invited so many guests that he blocked off the narrow street to his house and hired valets and security guards to park cars and make sure only invited guests were admitted. He had gone to great expense in providing fine food, an open bar, live entertainment and dancing. He let the guests know there were silver trays of cocaine upstairs for them to sample. To top things off, he had an elaborate casino setup, complete with dealers who were selling chips. She had attended with Luis and enjoyed playing detective, trying to observe everything she thought might be of interest to me.

Near midnight, when the party was really rocking, there was a raid. Plainclothes officers crashed through the front door and the guests fled in a panic, many running out the back across the patio and down the hillside toward the strip. Cathy said it was a funny sight to see: folks rolling down the hill in their fine gowns and tuxedos. Officers took a number of people to the sheriff's station. Most were released, but Luis had been booked for possession. Jaden was taken to the station but not booked, which she didn't understand. She told me the real reason she had tried to call me so quickly, was because Jaden was saying the raid was my fault. He believed that I had visited him earlier that day in order to set up the raid and that the interview was only a ruse.

My hope of irritating Jaden was having the desired effect. Jaden's fear was causing him to attribute to me the events in his life that I had nothing to do with. A good detective shoots for that kind of an advantage as it provides a great deal of leverage to play with. However, I had no idea who conducted the raid.

Krissy said she asked at West Hollywood what agency had conducted the raid, because she also thought I was behind it. When she didn't see me there, she tried to contact me by phone.

I really appreciated Krissy's help, but to find out about the raid in this manner was disappointing. I hung up wishing I could have been there. It would have given me a perfect excuse to search the house for any clues about Max's murder.

I drove to the sheriff's station that evening, confident that if they were behind the raid they would have told me it was coming. I wanted to introduce myself to Luis.

I was directed to Luis' cell. He was friendly, and we chatted about the party, his arrest, and Max. He gave me the same story that Krissy had about last seeing him at a club on the Strip. He added nothing beyond that and said he had dropped Max off outside of Krissy's apartment after they left the club. Luis said Max was a friend of Jaden. He admitted that it was strange that Jaden had not once brought up Max's death to him.

He claimed to know nothing about the raid that took place. I couldn't tell if he was lying, so I played along and asked if he would take a polygraph exam in order for me to eliminate him as a suspect in Max's murder. He refused, but it didn't upset me; I just told him that it was his call and that I would withhold any help I could give him on his arrest as long as he chose not to cooperate with me.

I always kept my word when talking to possible suspects, so I was careful never to bluff or make claims of some action that I would not, or could not follow up on if challenged. I already knew most suspects were going to test me whenever I did make a threat or an offer of help. I checked Luis's booking slip and wrote down the address that he listed for his residence. It was in Hollywood just like Krissy had told me.

Before leaving the station, I found out from the detectives that the raid was conducted by the DEA. That was a mystery to me. I was running behind on getting records and backgrounds on all the people I was meeting, but I had obtained Jaden's rap sheet before going to interview him and noticed that he had served time in federal prison. Maybe the feds were paying attention to him. Whatever, I knew it was something for me to check out.

● ● ● ● ●

I called Krissy to let her know that I had talked to Luis and that he was not aware that I had contacted her. I warned her to be careful what she said around him and Jaden. I knew she felt confident about dealing with people from her years of experience as a prostitute. But I told her she was dealing with an increased danger if anyone thought she was cooperating with me, especially if Jaden or Luis were involved in the murder as I suspected. I felt it was my responsibility to protect her. I assumed this responsibility with all witnesses. I didn't make them false promises of help and was determined to do my best to protect them. I guess I had a thing for good customer service.

Krissy decided to move for her own protection because too many people knew where she lived. She made it clear that she trusted Luis more than Jaden and she was certain Luis would not have been involved in Max's murder. "They were best friends," she told me. "Luis is a small time dealer compared to Jaden." That's when she told me that Jaden and Hannah not only sold heroin, they were addicts with very big habits.

On Monday morning I was advised by the coroner's investigator that he had made a positive identification on John Doe. His name was Charles, and all pertinent information had been forwarded to my friend at Rampart Detectives. Rampart had not contacted me or RHD which meant they were going to work the case. Still, I could not put Charles out of my mind and made a mental note to find out from Bob the particulars of that investigation.

I started the week getting more information on Max. Krissy had spoken to his mother by phone. She lived in the Chicago area. Krissy had advised her of Max's death after she was visited by the West Valley detectives. She gave me the phone number. This was a phone call I did not look forward to making, so I took some time with a donut to think about what I was going to say. Krissy told me that Max was Rose's only child. When I made the call and introduced myself, Rose started crying.

Our conversation turned out to be a lengthy one. Rose wanted to talk. She told me that she was a single mom who had lived alone since Max left home. It wasn't hard to imagine how lonely she was feeling right then and I was more than willing to stay on the phone so she could talk as much as she wanted. What I couldn't realize at the time was that it was the beginning of what would become a personal friendship. She sounded like a sweetheart. She had raised Max in Joliet, living in the shadow of the prison. Max's dad was not involved in his life and was thought to have moved to Italy before Max was born. She never married and provided for the two of them by working as a registered nurse. She spoke several languages and was well known in her community for helping the underprivileged with health care. She described Max as any proud mother would, a good boy, good musician, good athlete, who grew to be a fine man. She said he had joined the Marines after high school. She described him as somewhat of a celebrity in the neighborhood. He had become a professional drummer and singer who mentored young musicians in Joliet.

Rose claimed to know nothing about Max's connection to drugs, and that made perfect sense. A son growing up knowing that in his mother's eyes he was the good son would learn to hide anything that would spoil the illusion. However, she choked up when she told me that he had stopped communicating with her after his discharge. "He had gotten mixed up with the wrong crowd playing music and I did not hear from him after he moved to California. He just recently called me and said he missed me and wanted to be a better son. I have not seen him for too many years," she blurted through her sobs.

Rose told me that Max's friends were starting to call as they found out about his death. I asked her to keep a journal of who called and what they had to say and I promised to stay in touch with her. At the end of the conversation, she said something that I didn't know how to respond to. She thanked me for calling her and said, "You sound like a man who knows God."

IV. _LUIS_

The way of the wicked is like darkness. They do not know over what they stumble. (Proverbs 4:19)

I talked to Krissy the next day. She had begun to report to me every couple of days. She had seen Luis when he was released from jail and said he cried like a baby because Max was dead. She was trying hard to convince me that she would know if he had anything to do with Max's murder. She also told me the address I had taken from his booking slip was where he lived, but that he kept his drugs in a stash pad he rented in West Hollywood. She said he was careful to conceal the location of his drug stash from everyone. He didn't want to have to relocate it, so it was a secret he guarded closely. I realized then how involved she was with Luis. She told me she would give me the stash pad address if I would come by her new apartment the next morning. She had moved into Hollywood.

It was mid-morning when I arrived at Krissy's. I knocked loudly, but there was no response. I waited. She finally shouted that she had heard me. She slurred her words and I figured she must be hung over. When she finally opened the door, she looked like she'd had a rough night. Her hair was in her eyes, and her make-up looked like it was from the night before. She was completely naked. She signaled for me to follow her and she flopped down on the sofa in the living room.

We had met often enough for her to be aware that I always kept my eyes on her face. I was careful never to lower my eyes to her body the way her clients did. She had even asked me once if I thought her body was ugly. I was able to avoid an answer, but I was confident she knew she was attractive. After all, her business is quite competitive.

But her question caused me to reflect on why I was careful not to look at the bodies of the women I met on my cases, especially prostitutes. Even though it looked like a noble thing, I was aware that I was trying to prove I could be as strong as my dad. His

39

words, "Never show weakness," were behind my commitment to always be aware of my eyes. I never wanted a woman to see me as some weak man who drooled over her body. It seemed obvious to me that Krissy enjoyed knowing she could trust me that way and it showed in her conversation. She freely talked about personal and confidential things that could be dangerous for her if I ever broke her confidence.

However, her being naked was something new for me to consider. I thought she might be giving me the big test, to see if I would fall for some fast sex or at least scope out the view she was offering. I reminded her of the purpose of my visit, and she jumped up and went into her bedroom. I got the feeling she was upset.

Krissy brought out an address book and wrote down the address of Luis' stash pad. I told her that as long as she had her book, she might as well provide me with the names of her regular clients. She gave me the book and told me I could make my own copy. As I left, she followed me to the door, still undressed, and asked me if I was happily married. She would tell me on a later occasion how much she despised the men she satisfied sexually, men whom she saw as so weak they would sell their soul just to get her to pretend she desired them. "I know how to make them feel like I want them so much they'll pay me any price I ask, but it's always about what satisfies them. They never care about me or how I feel," were the words of a lonely party girl facing a moment of reality.

Yet, Krissy still spoke of being madly in love with Max. I wondered if she was just trying to convince herself that if she wanted, she could find a meaningful relationship.

Luis had a record of arrests for drug possession but no convictions. He was always represented by the same defense attorney, a man who was well known for representing celebrities and organized crime figures against narcotics charges. His specialty was pleading out his clients to lesser charges than what they had been arrested for. The guilty plea usually kept them from serving jail time. The attorney, a small man with the appearance of a weasel, had become wealthy and arrogant by arranging plea deals. The courts and

DA's office seemed willing to go along with his acting as a mediator in criminal cases. I guess everyone was looking for the easy way out.

Krissy told me that the girls included him on a list they called the horny lawyers club. He and a couple of other lawyers hung out with the working girls and would represent them if they got busted. The cost was sexual favors each time the lawyers visited, and she said it was often.

I spent the next few days running police and phone records and searching through field interview cards at various police stations. Field interview cards, referred to as FI cards, are filed whenever a person is contacted by the police. They contain the person's name, physical description, and contact information. FI cards contain information that is occasionally invaluable. I found no FI's on Max or any of the people I had thus far encountered.

I received a message that Rose had tried to contact me at RHD. It had been a week since I first spoke with her. When I called, she was quite upset. She told me that she had received a call from one of Max's musician friends telling her that he had been castrated and his penis placed in his mouth. She told me that she trusted me to tell her the truth about this. I had received the autopsy report, so I told her I would call her right back. I pulled the report from my file. I called Rose and read from it, "the penis and scrotum are markedly decomposed and swollen." She agreed that the report would have noted any mutilation. I told her I would send her a copy of the report, if she wished. I knew she would understand the medical jargon it contained. She seemed embarrassed that she had believed a rumor. She gave me the caller's name and contact information so I could follow up. When I did, it was easy to tell this guy was full of beans. I warned him not to bother Rose again.

I found myself wishing I could do something to help Rose. It sounded as if she had no close friends or family and limited finances. She sounded so soft-hearted that I guessed she was an easy target for folks looking for someone to take advantage of. I surprised myself by inviting her to come to Los Angeles. I told her she could stay at my house, and I would take her to the location where Max's body had been found. This seemed very important to her, and she was eager to accept my invitation. The timing would depend on her work schedule.

The week allowed me more time to continue my investigation of the Bible. By the following weekend, I had read the beginning story so many times that I was starting to imagine being in the garden myself. As I read on, determined to finish the entire Bible, I found that I was tracking themes that began in the garden story. I had even started keeping notes the way I did with my cases.

After going to bed on Friday night, I was awakened by that dreaded phone call obscenely shouting that I was not allowed to sleep. It is rarely good news when the phone rings in the middle of the night. Fear tells everyone that this is the call we don't want to answer, the nightmare call. For a homicide detective, the fear of personal bad news is replaced with the knowledge that, no matter how tired we are, we will not be going back to sleep. It always means a forced awakening to dress and drive to a death scene to examine something so repulsive that it would haunt a normal person for a long time.

However, I was surprised when I answered this call. It was from the West Hollywood narcotics officer who knew Luis. I had given him my home number in case he came up with anything he thought might be helpful in my investigation. He informed me that Luis had been in a shoot-out earlier in the evening, and he had been booked in the West Hollywood jail for assault with a deadly weapon. The detective summarized the situation, "He was in an argument with one of his drug clients over a debt that was owed him. The client threatened to kick his ass. Luis is not a fighter, and decided he would outrun his client. He quickly discovered that his client was not just stronger, but he was faster. As his client closed in on him, he tried something novel. He tried shooting backward while running forward. His shot ricocheted off the sidewalk into the doper's ankle. When the doper fell, Luis went back and started searching the guy's pockets looking for the money he was owed. Problem was, one of our black and whites rolled up just in time to stop Luis and take him into custody. The story came from the other guy who's in the hospital now."

I decided that, as much as I hated waking up, I did not want to miss this opportunity. I quickly dressed and headed for West Hollywood. I had promised my lieutenant that I would take Matt along whenever I was going into the field on this case, so I called Matt at home and he said he would meet me at the West Hollywood station. The narcotics detective was waiting for me. I got there ahead of Matt and pulled Luis' property from the jailer.

When a prisoner is booked, his property is itemized in his presence, sealed in a plastic bag and filed. It is then sent with him if he is transferred to court, or returned to him if he is released. Luis' property consisted of the usual personal items a man carries in his pockets. One thing that I noticed right away was that he had given a different residence address on his booking slip from the one he had used last time. He had guessed at an address in the San Fernando Valley and he had guessed wrong. I knew the address did not exist.

When Matt arrived, I asked him if he cared if I interviewed Luis alone. Matt seemed relieved. I asked the narcotics detective to pull Luis out of his cell and place him in an interrogation room. Luis almost seemed happy to see me again. I kept our conversation light, kidding him about the shooting. "Were you trying to be like the good cowboy who never shot to hurt the bad guy, only to knock the gun out of his hand?" He asked me what I meant. "I thought you might have been trying to shoot the shoelaces out of your friend's shoes when you realized he was outrunning you." He laughed and asked me if I would work for him collecting debts from anyone bigger than he. "Unless you start selling dope to jockeys, that would be everyone you deal with," I threw back at him.

"Maybe you could help me become the dealer to the jockeys," he said. I told him that would still be a problem for him. "Jockeys may be small but they are tough guys. If you were lucky enough to whip one, everyone would laugh at you for picking on a little guy and if the jockey kicked your ass like I think he would, then you would be…well, you'd be Luis."

As the conversation turned to the more serious aspects of his shooting, he rationalized the incident by making himself the victim. "It was really just a misunderstanding," he finished. I asked him how long he had lived at the address on his booking slip, the one in the Valley. He looked at me quizzically, revealing he had already forgotten the address he gave the jailer when he was booked. I placed his property bag on the table and removed the keys. Then he told me he had just moved and it was a new address. I asked him which key opened the door and he picked one from the key ring. I told him I still considered him a suspect in Max's murder and since he didn't want to take a lie detector test, that I would be satisfied if I could search his residence for clues. "If I don't find anything, I'll stop bothering you."

He was eager to agree to that. I took a piece of paper and wrote, "I hereby give my permission to RHD detectives to search my residence. I am giving him the key." He signed and dated the statement, and I left with his key ring.

I thanked the detective who had called me and drove to the address that Krissy had given me for Luis' stash pad with Matt in tow. I only told Matt that Luis had given us permission to search his place.

• • • • •

The stash pad was in a large apartment building not far from the sheriff's station, so it only took a few minutes to get there. Luis' apartment was on the second floor. I found the right key to unlock the door. I thought I saw the window curtains move in the adjacent apartment, but figured it was just a nosey neighbor.

The stash pad was a one bedroom with a kitchenette. It was nearly unfurnished and far too neat for anyone to be living there. The walls were bare and there were no pictures or knickknacks anywhere. On a counter between the kitchen and living room were a mirror and scales with white powder residue on both. A telephone was also on the counter. I copied the number and went to the bedroom. It consisted of a neatly made bed and a dresser.

Matt was following me as I did a walk through. I pulled open the top drawer in the bedroom dresser. It was full of neatly rolled plastic tubes, each containing white powder. I was looking at Luis's cocaine stash. The large drawer was packed so tightly that I couldn't see to the bottom. Matt was looking over my shoulder. I was waiting for a reaction from him when we were interrupted by a loud knock on the front door. I closed the dresser drawer, and went back to the living room. I cracked open the front door, surprised to see two uniformed sheriff's deputies.

Krissy had told me that she thought Luis paid a neighbor to keep an eye out for anyone snooping around his apartment and once again, her information was confirmed. I stepped outside onto the landing. I was thinking that it might be a good thing to let the spy get a look at me. His description would assure Luis that I had been to his stash pad.

I did worry about the uniformed officers. It would be really awkward if they wanted to come inside the apartment. I identified myself and told them I was conducting a search and that the West Hollywood detectives had been notified. They were very respectful and asked no questions. They said a neighbor had made an anonymous call that prowlers were at the apartment. Then they left.

When I stepped back inside the apartment, I could see that Matt was becoming unnerved. I told him I wanted to finish searching the bedroom. I made sure he saw the cocaine and asked him if he could evaluate what we had found. Like me, Matt had no experience working narcotics so both of us were clueless as to the amount and value of the drugs.

I opened the drawer below the one that held the cocaine. It was full of currency, neatly stacked in bundles, most appearing to be twenties and hundreds. I think Matt broke sweat as I removed the drawer with the cash. He really didn't know me well, and I figured he was wondering if I was going to pocket the cash. Narcotics detectives are commonly confronted with this type of situation, sometimes involving millions of dollars. The reason LAPD was corruption free was because only the best applicants were hired with no exceptions. And character was a priority of the very thorough background investigation that was conducted on each of us. We all believed in doing our duty with integrity and none of us would tolerate corruption or theft or accepting bribes. Each officer would view any such act as a personal betrayal. The result was that there was no corruption. I had no way of knowing that in a few short years the department would succumb to affirmative action regulations that would change all of this.

I dumped the cash in the middle of the bed. Next, I did the same with the drawer full of cocaine. Now I faced a serious moment that I had not encountered before in my special assignment at RHD. I had a partner who was also a witness. I had no idea that my next remark was going to rattle Matt, as I was both kidding and serious at the same time, "What I'm going to tell you now means that I will have to kill you." If I hadn't smiled, which I usually don't do, I think he would have run.

Since I worked my cases alone, decisions about arrests and evidence were easy to make and I never had to worry about being contradicted in court. I had successfully solved a number of cases since my arrival at RHD, giving me experience at what to expect in court. Many RHD detectives did not have this experience because they were not solving cases.

I showed Matt the note Luis had signed and explained how I had tricked Luis into signing it. I told him that I would never put a witness or informant at risk, so we would have to agree to a story that would explain how we found the stash pad while doing our best to protect Krissy. This would be necessary if we were to book the money and dope as evidence. He looked at the paper with Luis' signature and I could tell he understood why I hadn't put an address on the note.

I told him I knew Luis' attorney and had watched him in court, attempting to split the testimony of officers. He would put all the pressure he could on officers hoping for the slightest discrepancy in their testimony. I told Matt I wanted to book the narcotics and the cash and charge Luis. I would call the sheriff's narcotics detective to help us with the evidence and arrest. Making the arrest would allow me to put incredible pressure on Luis to cooperate with me in the murder case. I told Matt, "I will testify that when Luis signed the note, he also gave me his address and the key. It will be hard to refute my testimony since there will be no other way to explain how we got here."

I told Matt how I would use the arrest to squeeze Luis because once I had him in my custody, I could make other arrests threatening to reveal that he was my informant. Luis would want to cooperate and have me protect him, rather than become my adversary and have me lay him out as a snitch, especially if he knew what happened to Max. I took the time to go over all of this in detail with Matt, assuring him that I would never waiver on my story. "If there's any doubt in your mind whether you can hold up in this plan, you are free to tell me now and we'll make another plan that you are comfortable with. Don't you dare put me at risk by making a half-hearted agreement. The day will come when you're alone on the witness stand and you'll be under attack to see if you'll crack."

I didn't know what court experience Matt had. Perhaps he didn't understand what I was telling him. His face gave me the answer before he spoke and I knew I could not risk doing my job with someone who might make a mistake that could jeopardize my career. Matt confirmed this by saying he was just going to leave and go back home, and I could tell him later what I decided to do. As he left he said, "I hope you don't arrest Luis." I assured him that I would make a different plan and no one would know what happened except the two of us. What wasn't said, but what I assumed we both understood, was that we could never work together again. I liked Matt and respected his decision.

Before I left the apartment, I took one of the tubes of cocaine and dumped it into the toilet so that Luis would see it floating. I knew if I flushed all the dope, Luis's life would probably be over. I was trying to decide how I could turn Luis into an informant, so I left the dope and the cash on the bed. I would tell the Sheriff's narcotics detective what I had found and allow him to decide how to take down Luis.

I dropped off Luis' keys at West Hollywood without seeing him. The detectives told me that Luis had posted bail and would be processed for release. I asked them to give him my business card with the phone number for DHQ. Then I started to drive home. After all the excitement, I was starting to feel tired but before I got very far I realized that if Luis went to his stash pad and saw what I had done, he would be calling me right away. I decided to go for a donut and wait for a while. I waited through more than one donut, a couple of cups of black coffee and a Kahlua cigar. The call from DHQ finally came, telling me they had received an emergency call from a guy named Luis. He had left the number for the phone in his stash pad.

Luis was so panicky when I called, that his voice cracked. "Are you crazy? Are you trying to get me killed or are you waiting outside to do it yourself when I walk out?" he said, choking up as he sputtered out the words.

I reminded him of my warning that he would have to choose whether or not he was going to help me solve Max's murder. I told him that in a few minutes I was going to call him back to meet me for the polygraph test he had earlier refused. "There's no way I'm walking out of this place," he responded, "I know you have me surrounded by narcs just waiting for me to come out."

I told him he could choose not to take the test, and I'd have the narcs break down the door and take him into custody. "You'd better start flushing your stuff now if you make that decision." I paused, waiting for his answer, realizing that sometimes I did try a bluff, but Luis had set up this bluff by believing I was waiting outside for him. He told me he would take the lie detector test.

It only took a few minutes for the Van Nuys Scientific Investigation Division to locate a polygraph operator, and they assured me he would be ready within the hour. I called Luis back and told him I would be waiting for him at the front desk of Van Nuys Division. I warned him not to tell anyone what was happening for his own safety. He said he was on the way and pleaded with me to call off the narcs that he was still convinced I had watching his stash pad. "I don't want these guys coming into my apartment after I leave."

• • • • •

The polygraph is used to exert pressure. Since it is not admissible in court, it doesn't really matter what the test results are, just how the operator and the detective work together to make the test effective. A good operator knows how to make a suspect think the machine is producing the evidence that the detective wants. The detective can then put pressure on a suspect to see if he will break or if he proves himself truthful. That is the real test. Throughout the extensive test, which I was monitoring from another room, Luis remained consistent in his statements that he was not present when Max was killed. The machine showed a questionable reading when he was asked if he knew who had killed Max. The operator was someone I trusted to do a good examination and he told me it was his opinion that Luis was being truthful. I agreed.

I took Luis to an interrogation room and told him that unless he pissed backward on me, I would trust him. He was to report to me regularly and keep me apprised of what he found out about the murder, especially what he heard from Jaden and Hannah. He confirmed what Krissy had said, that both Jaden and Hannah were hooked on heroin and both had big habits. He also decided to give me more information that he had been withholding. Jaden was a major heroin dealer. His suppliers were a Mexican cartel that brought the dope to his house. He then arranged for a courier to deliver the heroin to Detroit. Luis said he was afraid of some of the guys Jaden hung out with, "They look mean and sometimes act as his bodyguards." He said some were blacks and others were Italians. He cautioned me that Jaden hated me and thought I was out to get him. The raid had embarrassed him and he was paranoid wondering what I was going to do next. His final bit of information was hard to believe, "Jaden has told me more than once that he's a made member of the Cosa Nostra. I've seen him with one of the Italian guys that he says is his boss, a guy he calls Charley. The black guy he hangs with is named Don. He told me Don belongs to the Black Muslims."

V. *ROSE*

Faithful are the wounds of a friend, but deceitful are the kisses of an enemy. (Proverbs 27:6)

We lived in a modest house, my wife, my daughter, and my three sons. Squeezing Rose in for a visit was not as easy as I thought it would be, but rarely was anything in my life as easy as it looked when I planned it. Rose turned out to be a very large woman of over 300 pounds, and my daughter's room was the smallest bedroom in our three bedroom house. Besides that, there was only one bed and my daughter had agreed, under compulsion and before we saw Rose, to share her bed. As soon as my daughter saw Rose I knew what was going through her mind and I was expecting her to volunteer to sleep in the garage. But Rose was amazingly gracious. She was sensitive to respecting my daughter and her property. She even offered, in front of my daughter, to stay at a hotel. I knew she couldn't afford that, but it said a lot about Rose. Although we were taken aback at her size, she made a hit with all of us and my daughter was sweet enough to insist that Rose stay in her room.

I remember reading once that denial is a better way of living. As a man approaching 40, I believed that I was over my insecurities about being a disappointment to my dad. He grew up through the depression in a family of one dozen children that included seven boys. Grandpa held a low-income job with the railroad, but it provided steady income in hard times. Grandma raised the kids. I felt privileged to sit in on many story-telling sessions with my dad and his brothers and being treated as if I was one of the boys by grandma. Those stories were often about hard times, but they were never told as stories of being poor or suffering. They were remembered as challenges to be faced and laughed about. It inspired me to belong to such a close-knit family who fought the battles of life together. There was never a story told that included betrayal of, or by, any family member toward another.

When the older brothers went to fight in WWII, there would be even more stories for me to absorb after they returned. After the war, the family was together again and in the eyes of this child, we were the perfect family and I had the perfect dad. In most of the stories of fights, especially on the streets of what today would be considered a ghetto, my dad was the hero, the rescuer, the one who showed up to protect his brothers and the family honor. I idolized my father as if he was Superman. I had even seen him box and play other sports, and I never saw him lose at anything. I wanted so badly for him to be proud of me that I would write notes to him about how much I loved him. I gave him pictures and cards that I drew while he was serving in the Navy.

But my dad was not a personal man. In his silence, I was left to develop my own beliefs, conclusions that were developed through the eyes of a child. The one that hit me hardest was that my dad was ashamed of me, that he saw a flaw in me that kept him distant.

His disappointment was not expressed in words; it was in his look and in his silence. One day when I was seven or eight, he brought me a present. It was really rare for my dad to bring home a gift, so it was especially significant that he did it for me and I was pumped. I opened the package to find a pair of boxing gloves. My first thought brought a big smile to my face. My dad was going to teach me how to box and he was the man who could beat up everyone. Superman was going to teach me how to fight. I tried to give him a hug, but he pushed me back and put the gloves on me.

After I had the gloves on, and still without saying a word, he took me to the front door. I looked through the screen door to see our neighbor, a man my dad despised because my dad couldn't tolerate weak men. The neighbor was with his son who was my age, but bigger and I perceived, stronger. I was small for my age. The neighbor's son was also wearing boxing gloves and smiling at me as he waited next to his dad. I knew for certain that I was about to get pounded into the ground and I was afraid. The only energy I could find was the energy to run. On the other side of our house from the neighbor was a wooded area. I burst through the screen door and ran into the woods where I hid.

My dad didn't call to me or look for me, and he never again spoke to me about the incident. When I snuck back into the house, I put the gloves back in the box and never wore them again. It had to be an embarrassing moment for dad, a man whom never backed down from anyone. Since he never spoke about what he saw in me, I came up with the name myself. After that day, I knew I was a coward. I didn't realize at the time how that word would determine the course of my life.

Dad never acknowledged my love notes, never said he loved me, and never offered any affection, not even a hug. My mom had been the safe one to get close to, but she fell ill when I was 18 and died within a few months. She was 38 years old. One of the things she did that left a big impression on me was when dad was away in the Navy. She knelt with me next to her bed and taught me how to pray.

• • • • •

So becoming a policeman and being allowed to work this special assignment became my way of proving to my dad that I wasn't a coward. Consumed by my work, I had neglected to see that my wife and my daughter had started to develop a rivalry for my attention. My daughter was now 14 and as the acrimony built, they became enemies. It was demanded of me to resolve tensions when I was home, something I didn't understand, even though I thought I knew everything. I was sure the problem was my wife, so I pressured her to handle the home life without my involvement. I thought my mom had done this while my dad was always absent, so it made perfect sense to me.

But my efforts to convince my wife that she was the adult only increased her anger. It seemed to me that she was being unfair by demanding so much from the kids, and then blaming it on me when it didn't work.

Being called to work, where I could control situations much better than at home, was an escape that I looked forward to. My daughter started calling me Dirty Harry after she saw the Clint Eastwood movie. My wife still calls me Rooster after the John Wayne character from True Grit. The lawman on horseback, who puts the reins in his mouth so he can put a gun in each hand and ride full speed toward the bad guys with guns blazing. These references felt good to me at the time, because it reinforced my attempts to portray myself as a hero instead of a coward. I didn't understand that to my wife and daughter it meant I was always running off to rescue someone, but it was never them. They saw the coward in me that I was trying to hide in my work, the one who failed to fight for them. I rationalized that I was just a typical hard-working guy providing for his family. I had become my dad.

Rose saw more of the family dynamics than I did. After staying at the house for a couple of days, I took her up to Mulholland Drive and showed her the spot where we had found Max. The hole was still in the ground. I stood by her while she wept. As I looked down into the canyon below the grave, I wondered if the killer might have been careless enough to throw something over the side. I was wearing boots with my Levis, so I started to climb down. It was so steep I couldn't keep from sliding, and then I saw some heavy vines that seemed to trail from the top down. I grabbed hold and used them to lower myself into the tree line below. Once there, I saw a shovel that had been thrown into a tree. I retrieved it and saw that it was the same brand as the axe that had been buried with Max. I climbed to the top and called for a photographer in order to get some pictures of where the shovel was found.

With the shovel secured in the trunk of my car, carefully handled with the hope of finding a fingerprint, Rose and I set out for home. On the way, Rose told me she was worried about the situation between my wife and daughter. I told her how much I appreciated her help and that I was aware of what she saw. I then excused my part in it by telling her that everything I had tried seemed to only make it worse. "Who do you talk to when you need help?" she asked. She looked so compassionate at that moment that I couldn't tell her I never needed help. "That's only for weak men," I heard my dad's voice in my head.

Rose persisted by telling me that she had put tremendous pressure on Max to come through for her, especially in light of all that she had sacrificed for him. "That's why he couldn't wait to join the Marines. And that's why we never spoke for years. Duke, what would you tell me to do, if I had him back for one last chance to talk?" I knew what I would tell her, but couldn't get the answer out because I knew I was failing to do it with my wife and daughter. So I remained silent, something that worked with everyone except my wife.

I was aware of a burning in my gut to prove myself by catching bad guys and protecting victims. I didn't know why, I just knew if I was pressed to choose, I would choose what I did as a homicide detective over anything else in life, and no one ever pressed me to make the choice. Maybe they already knew what my answer would be.

● ● ● ● ●

Little did I know at the time that I would need a nurse the very next day. The vines I had used for ropes turned out to be poison oak. The next morning I awoke with blisters on my arms and legs. My wife and Rose doctored me up and I left for work smelling like a pharmacy. I couldn't conduct interviews in my condition, so I headed to Jaden's place.

I had been spending every moment I could find in front of Jaden's house. The hillside homes have narrow, winding roads, and I found a spot to sit where Jaden would see me every time he left the house. There was only one way off the hill and I could see his jaws tighten every time he passed by me. He couldn't bring himself to look at me and would keep his eyes straight ahead, hands tightly gripping the steering wheel.

An unintentional benefit to this was that the couriers of his heroin had become aware of my presence and had stopped making deliveries to him. Maybe it was because I would stand outside of my car with my jacket off so my gun and badge were showing, who knows? I would then make it obvious that I was writing down the license number of every car that passed by. After about a week of this, Luis and Krissy told me that Jaden was consumed with how much he hated me. Not only was I cutting into his income, but he and Hannah had asked Luis to help them find a source to feed their personal habits.

Luis kept reminding me that he understood what Jaden was going through. "You are a pain in the ass, Duke. That dope you dumped in the toilet cost me twenty grand."

I had also been waving to Hannah whenever she left the house. On occasion, I would follow her or Jaden just to drive them a little closer to the edge. On one such occasion I thought I had pushed Jaden over. When he couldn't shake me, he started doing wheelies in the middle of Ventura Boulevard in the valley. In the traffic mess he created, he was able to speed away in a panic.

I was also making some time at home with Rose and my wife. Rose was very curious about my investigation of the Bible. She loved talking to me about it, and had a beautiful way of drawing me into conversation. She did it with questions, as if I had the answers to everything. I actually believed I did have the answers to everything, but not when it came to the bible. I figured Rose was the one with those answers and I was learning from her. She admitted that she read the Bible on her own just as I was doing, and tried to follow it faithfully in spite of her religion's neglect of it. She was raised a Roman Catholic. She asked me one day if I felt I had anything to do with God or Him with me. I avoided giving her an answer as I still wasn't sure what I believed. I was aware that I was getting close to the point where a decision would be required, but I still wasn't sure what it would be. I was already in my second reading of the whole Bible. I could make a lot of progress reading while sitting outside of Jaden's house. The message was clear to me that the Scriptures claimed to be God's word and could not be separated from Him. I was also intrigued that it said only a few people were going to end up with Him. I certainly didn't understand everything I was reading, but I couldn't stop. One day on that hill in West Hollywood I looked up to the sky and smiled, telling Him that He seemed to have hooked me and I felt He was reeling me in.

•••••

Rose wanted to see Krissy before she returned home. I made arrangements and we met Krissy for dinner at a restaurant near the beach. I didn't realize that they had never met before. I could see right away there was a tension between them. Rose went silent, and Krissy became aggressive. Krissy was upset over things that Max had told her about his mom's controlling ways. She had apparently tried to tell this to Rose over the phone and Rose would have none of it, blaming Max's downward life style on bad friends. Krissy had taken those remarks to include her.

I observed and learned some things I didn't know about Max. Since he grew up without a dad, Rose had stirred an interest in him for music and acting. She gave him drum lessons starting at four, and he had a rhythm that seemed to come from his heart. In elementary school, he was being asked to perform at events. She bought him a replica of one of the Cuban outfits that Ricky wore on the "I Love Lucy" show. His popularity soared with his imitations of Ricky and when the show was brought to Chicago for a taping, Ricky and Lucy arranged to have Max on the set. They loved him and he appeared in some of the shows, playing their son. Rose was sure they must have stayed in touch with him after he moved to California. It made Max so well known that his band was signing for shows all over the country.

Once Max had tasted Hawaii on one of his deployments with the Marines, he talked about opening his own club there someday. After his discharge, Rose said he left Joliet to join a black band in Philadelphia. When he came back, he said he was leaving for the west coast and she lost contact with him.

Krissy had brought a tape of Max's music that he recorded in a studio. Rose had never heard it. I asked Rose to leave it with me so I could make a copy. I wanted to see if there might be a clue on the tape and I was also curious to hear the music that Max played.

Krissy then asked Rose why she thought Max had tried to regain contact with her before his death. Rose did not know that it had happened at the urging of Krissy. She expressed to Rose how much in love they were and that she had become pregnant with his child before they had one of their many break-ups. She had miscarried. "When he found me this last time, he asked me to marry him," Krissy told Rose. Now they were holding one another and crying, "I never got to tell him yes."

As in most of my murder cases, I was getting to know the victim after his life had ended, in some ways better than the folks who loved him while he was alive. I frequently found myself with some dark secret about a victim's personal life that I could never disclose to the family.

Krissy had already given me the name of Max's agent and I had learned from him that Max had changed dramatically in the past year. The agent said he had found plenty of work for Max, but that for the past year Max refused to perform. Krissy had given me an address book that Max carried and from the notations, I figured Max had been dealing drugs for quite a while. I had not found out where he was living when he was killed, but Krissy had confirmed the clothes he was wearing were ones she had given him.

● ● ● ● ●

Rose left to return home the next day. She didn't have much money and other than her work, no reason to stay in Joliet. My wife and I invited her to consider moving to California and she said she would think about it. We told her we would build an addition to our house so she could live with us, but still have her own privacy. Of course, we had no idea how we would do this, but we cared about Rose.

After she left, Alice seemed more depressed than ever. Rose had set aside time just for her before leaving and I realized my daughter must have felt as if she was losing someone who was giving her the attention she wasn't getting from me or my wife. I never spoke to Rose again without her asking me about Alice. I believed Rose every time she assured me that she was praying for us daily.

I quickly got busy with my plan to continue harassing Jaden and Hannah, believing more than ever that they were responsible for Max's death. Within a couple of days I got a surprise. I watched Jaden leave the house one morning, but I remained parked outside. Before he returned, Hannah left the house and as she drove past me she stopped. She told me she had something important to tell me, but she was terrified of Jaden. She said some of the neighbors bought drugs from him and if they saw her talking to me, she would be in danger. She told me Jaden was leaving town soon and asked if she could meet with me while he was gone. I gave her my card with the number for DHQ and told her I'd be waiting for her call. To my surprise, the call came the next evening.

VI. *AMBUSH*

(The Scriptures) will keep you from the evil woman, from the smooth tongue of the adulteress. Do not desire her beauty in your heart, nor let her catch you with her eyelids. (Proverbs 6:24-25)

As the weekend began, I used it to catch up on some report writing. I had returned Krissy's trick book and she told me a bit about each guy   listed therein. She was sexually involved with a number of blacks that told her they were in the black mafia. She didn't know what that was, just said it was a term they used. She said they were well armed and wanted to pimp her out. On the opposite side, she had some Cosa Nostra family that she was sexually involved with and she said they wanted to pimp her out also. Her third connection was known as the queen of the Hollywood hookers. She gave me her name and number and told me she invites only the top girls to a meeting at her home in the Hollywood hills every month. "It's a chance to meet some high rollers," Krissy said, "I have met some of L.A.'s big shot politicians there."

She told me about a guy from Malibu who had taken her to Hawaii and wanted her to move in with him. While staying at his place, she said she looked through his library and found thousands of dollars stuffed between the pages of books. "Most of the girls I know would have ripped him off," she said, "but I didn't take anything because of my faith in God." I guess everyone has a moment when they want to believe they are right with the Lord.

The tension all of this created for Krissy was the threat of one side finding out about the other. Krissy said the Italians hated the blacks and told her, "We take a nigger with us on every job, just in case we get busted. That way, we've got somebody dumb to blame." She said the top Italian she knew was named Gordon and that he scared her once when he said, "If I ever find out that you're screwing a nigger, they'll find you cut up in little pieces." Krissy was definitely walking a tightrope. She had become a great informant for me. At least twice every week she would call and update me on what she was hearing on the street. She seemed to enjoy playing detective, but I worried about her safety.

I had also made a significant contact within DEA. While agencies were often at odds with one another, individuals were not and I was always looking for guys I could trust. Dave was one such agent.

Dave was at Jaden's party, having been tipped off by one of his DEA informants. He said it wasn't easy getting inside because Jaden had armed bodyguards posted outside. The layout was the biggest gambling operation Dave had ever seen in Los Angeles. He estimated that he saw over $50,000 in chips at one table alone. The bank was being kept upstairs.

Dave had ordered the raid and said they hadn't booked Jaden because the house was rented in the name of someone else. Dave told me he would introduce me to his informant to see if he could give me any help in my murder case. His informant on Jaden was the same one who had set up the buy-bust that led to the arrest of Max. Dave said Barry had his parole violated and was in custody at Terminal Island and available to be interviewed.

When I finished my report writing, I had a pretty long to-do list for the upcoming week. Before I could get back to my family, I received a call from West Valley. One of their patrol units had responded to an abandoned vehicle call not far from where Max's body was found. The responding officer discovered that the car had been reported stolen. When he searched the car, he found items with Max's name on them. The car had been impounded, so I told them I would take a look at it on Monday.

I actually initiated going to a church on Sunday morning. I chose one near my house because it had Bible in its name. I was in for two surprises. The speaker turned out to be a Jewish man who was standing in for the pastor. He unfolded the Old Testament to reveal something I had been looking for my entire life. All strength and power reside in God and the Scriptures identify Him as a warrior. Wow, how those words hit me. I had spent my life striving to be validated by the warrior-men in my family and now I had the opportunity to be validated by the ultimate warrior. The speaker went on to explain how the Lord uses his power to fight for love. His conclusion pointed to how His fight led to the crucifixion and resurrection defeated death. There was no doubt in my mind that I was ready to make a decision to give my life to this warrior who fought for me. I sought the speaker out after the service and he prayed with me about my decision.

The second surprise was to see the impact on my wife and kids from being in church. My wife met some very nice folks. I hadn't realized how lonely my wife was in my absence. Her only outside contact was her family. Her parents had told her she could never be successful unless she married a man with money. In that category, I was about as unsuccessful as they come and her parents made no secret that they despised me.

My only brother raised pit bulls and gave me one after I was married. After meeting my in-laws, he said, "Isn't it strange how carefully we check the pedigree of dogs to get some idea of behavior, yet when we marry we pay absolutely no attention to the lineage, as if it's not going to effect the behavior of our wives?"

● ● ● ● ●

I had graduated from high school at 6'2" and 154 pounds, a skinny, pimply beanpole. I began hanging out with weight lifters and became obsessed with developing an external strength that would hide the label of coward that had attached itself to me. It was in the gym that I began a friendship with a policeman who was going to influence me to enter law enforcement.

This Sunday at church, I realized I had been giving all of my attention to my physical being, which was going to get old and perish some day, while ignoring the personal part of me, that which could not be destroyed. I was determined to learn a workout routine that would strengthen my heart.

Sunday evening I put all serious thoughts behind me and at dinner time enjoyed having fun with my family. The kids had me laughing so hard that I rolled off my chair onto the floor and the milk came out of my nose. That started a contagious laughter that kept us going as everyone rolled around on the dining room floor. I announced that we were going out for ice cream after dinner.

Before we left the dinner table, I received a call from DHQ. Hannah had called and left a message that she could meet me tonight. My wife sighed hopelessly when the phone rang and then everyone drooped as I told them that I had to go to work. My daughter slouched away to her room. The boys wanted to go with me.

Whenever I got home before bedtime, I would park in the garage and sneak into the house. I loved to wait until I heard the boys running to find me. It didn't matter what they were doing, they would stop when they heard the garage door go up. I would ambush them by getting on my hands and knees and tackling them from a hiding place. I knew this night would be different since it was already getting late and I was just leaving. It was likely I wouldn't be back until morning, maybe not until they had left for school. I promised we would get ice cream the next night. It didn't help.

I had about an hour's drive to get to West Hollywood. My first stop was the Sheriff's station. Since no one at RHD would know I was in the field, I at least wanted to alert the sheriff's detectives. After telling the detective on duty about Hannah's call, I drove into the hills to Jaden's house by myself.

I had spent plenty of time scoping out the area. The left side of the house, as one faced the front door, was the downhill side. There was no neighboring residence on this side; it fell sharply into a small canyon full of trees and brush. On the uphill side there was a residence next door. There was also a neighbor across the street. Since the location was on a curve, not much could be seen beyond this.

It was completely dark when I arrived. An overcast sky blocked any light from the moon. As if she had been waiting for me, Hannah answered the door immediately when I knocked. She was dressed in a full length, white nightgown and robe.

I was expecting her to invite me in, but she claimed to have seen one of Max's associates patrolling the street before my arrival. She nervously looked out the door as if she was checking for traffic and asked where I had parked. She told me she was afraid to have me come inside in the event that when I left someone should see me.

I could see she was hyper, but overcame my doubts by attributing her attitude to the fear of talking to me. "The safest place to talk is the patio in back," she said as she pointed to the downhill side of the house. "There's a path over there. I'll meet you in back. No one can see us from the street." I knew she was right. In all the time I had staked out the front of the house, I was never able to see what was on the other side.

Stepping into the dark shadows on the downhill side of the house, I realized it was more treacherous than it appeared from the street. I had to hug the side of the house to keep from slipping down the hill. The further I inched my way toward the back of the house, the darker it got. I felt my way along until I could see the patio. There was a chain link fence on the side toward me. I got close enough to make out a gate next to the house, and the path I was on seemed to end there. The trees were set closer to the house as I neared the patio and I used them to balance myself as I squeezed my way toward the gate.

When I reached the patio, the moon broke through the clouds. I looked through the gate and saw that the patio contained a large pool. I could see Hannah watching for me from inside the house. When she saw me, she stepped out through the sliding patio door. The reflections from the moonlight bounced off the pool water as she walked toward me. It seemed surreal, with the light shimmering on her as she walked, like a scene from a black-and-white silent movie. Then I realized she was too white, looking more like a corpse.

She was wearing the same nightgown but without the robe. As she approached me, she slipped the nightgown off her shoulders, and let it slide to the ground. She continued to walk toward me in the nude.

As quickly as the moon had lighted the scene, it retreated behind the clouds and I was standing in the darkness trying to see what Hannah was going to do. "Something's wrong with this picture," my sub-conscience alerted me, yet I hesitated as if I needed to figure it out before acting.

Hannah continued toward me, ghost-like, and her appearance began to creep me out. I wondered if she had underestimated me in thinking I would fall into a sexual trap. But as she got close enough for me to make out the look on her face, I realized I was already in a trap. I had allowed her to draw me to a place where she could accuse me of stalking her. "Run, Duke," a voice inside me commanded. Hannah was nearing the gate. The narrow path I was on made it impossible to turn around, so I took a step backward.

I froze for an instant when I felt the gun barrel touch the back of my head. A reaction from my training at the police academy caused me to spin to my right with my right arm up in a blocking position. If the gunman was right-handed, and he always was in my training, I should be able to knock the gun away.

I never felt myself make contact with the gunman's arm, and the resulting blast knocked me over the hillside. I was sliding helplessly, feeling no pain, and wondering how much it was going to hurt when something stopped my slide. I had the sensation of being conscious, yet disconnected from my body. I was picking up speed while flailing my arms, trying to grab something that would slow my slide. Somewhere on that hillside the lights went out for me.

•••••

I could barely see as I opened my eyes. I was on my stomach with my face in the dirt. My eyes hurt because of the dust and my vision was distorted. I was startled to see that I was lying next to a grave and my heart started pounding as I wondered if I was dead. I blinked harder, trying to focus.

I was next to Max's grave. My view was partially blocked by two people kneeling next to the grave with their backs toward me. I rolled onto my side and got myself up on one elbow. I had a weird feeling that I shouldn't speak, so as quietly as I could I got to my feet.

I walked around the grave and saw Max's head protruding. The two strangers were groaning, as they rocked back and forth in obvious pain. The man was using his hands to dig a space around the head in the grave and when I looked closely, I saw that it was not Max. Everything else was the same, but the body in the grave. He was younger than Max, with long black hair. As the man gently lifted the head, I could even see the wound that was inflicted to the back of the head.

The man gently placed the boy's head down and embraced the woman. They wept together. I watched in silence, uncertain as to what I was witnessing.

The environment changed as the morning sun broke through. I was able to see more clearly now. The couple was still grieving. I saw that their faces were raw from crying. For the first time they seemed aware of my presence. They were crudely dressed in what appeared to be animal skins, yet they were both stunning in appearance. They were physically perfect, which was even more evident when they stood and I saw that they were much taller than I.

Without speaking, the man motioned for me to follow and they walked away from the grave toward a nearby hill. I followed, as they took a trail that led steeply uphill. The wind was still blowing hard, and it was very dry, scratching my throat. The couple kept looking back to see if I was keeping up with their pace. I could make out the trail, but they took such big strides that I felt like a kid trying to keep up with the big people. I was glad when I saw them stop at what appeared to be the crest of the hill. They watched me chug my way up to them. I tried to hide how hard I was breathing.

When I reached them, I was amazed at the view. It was spectacular! The sun was rising behind us and it dawned on the valley below. I squinted to see clearly. Below us was what looked like a densely wooded forest. Its beauty was captivating. It was so green and moist, that it sparkled like a beautiful jade in the morning sunlight. I was afraid of heights, but without realizing it I moved to the very edge of the hill to take in all that I could. I saw a river twisting through the trees of the forest, but I couldn't see where it began or ended. The terrain outside and around the perimeter of the forest was sandy-dry and harsh looking.

The couple motioned for me to proceed down the hill, pointing to an overgrown path leading toward the forest. It was clear that they were urging me to go there. I asked them what this was about, but they only stared at me. I asked them what had happened to the young man in the grave. Again, I was met with stares and silence. I pulled out my police identification, something I rarely did, and I showed it to them. Their reaction was the same. I concluded that they were deaf and dumb, or just plain dumb, but I wasn't about to go down that path without knowing what the purpose was.

I motioned for my new friends to go with me. They started and stopped more than once, but slowly took the lead down the hillside.

Before we left this vista, I took a close look around at where we stood. The spot was well worn. Rocks had been carefully placed where the couple could sit and view the scene below. "These folks have spent a lot of time sitting up here; I wonder what it means to them?" I thought as I started down the path, unaware that they had been looking for far more than just the beautiful view.

● ● ● ● ●

We approached the east side of the garden. When we were about 100 yards away, I saw someone standing at the forest edge. He appeared dangerous, very tall and standing at attention. I thought he should be wearing Marine dress blues. The couple froze when they saw the stranger. I saw that he was holding a sword in his right hand.

The man I had been following slowly approached the stranger. I thought I heard my friend speak to the sentry. I couldn't understand what was being said. "No wonder they didn't speak to me, they don't speak English," I told to myself. The stranger with the sword looked menacing to me and the closer my friend got, the more intense the situation looked.

Then the stranger made a sudden move toward my friend. "He brought me here for protection," I thought. I instinctively reached for my sidearm. Against LAPD rules, I carried a .45 automatic. Since I worked alone, I had asked a firearms expert at the academy the best weapon to carry, and he told me that the department authorizes SWAT to carry the .45 auto. I justified doing the same because my assignment was a dangerous one and I worked alone. I didn't holster the .45, but kept it tucked inside the waist of my pants. Now, when I reached for it, it wasn't there. I remembered sliding down the hill and figured it had fallen from my waist. I still had my police ID, so I held it up and approached the Marine sentry.

When he saw me coming toward him, he put his hands on the shoulders of my friend and pushed him away from the forest entrance. I stopped in disbelief when I saw that the sword did not fall to the ground when the sentry let go of it. Instead, it started flashing brightly as if the sun was reflecting lightning bolts from it. The sword started moving toward me on its own, ahead of the sentry. My friend retreated to his wife and they started to walk away from me.

"Wait," I shouted at them. I thought I was must be hallucinating as I heard myself shout, "Adam! Eve! Is this the garden of the Lord?"

They walked faster toward the path that would take them back up the hillside without looking back at me. One thing that I was not imagining was the sword, it looked razor sharp and lethal.

I decided to retreat with my friends, but before I could catch up with them the sentry caught me from behind. His grip was so powerful that he lifted my feet off the ground. "What a way for me to end," I gulped, "I always dreamed of going out in a blaze of glory, but now I'm going to vanish from the face of the earth with no one to know what happened to me."

As danger closed in on me, I mustered all the energy I could and I shouted, "God, if you are there, this officer needs help!"

VII. *THUNDER*

And I heard a voice from heaven, like the sound of many waters and like the sound of loud thunder... (Revelation 14:2)

The loudest thunder I ever heard was in North Dakota. It was late in the evening and I was standing with my dad in the shelter of a dog racing track when a bolt of lightning startled the crowd. It turned night into day, a spectacular bright light that smashed to the ground. When the thunder rolled in behind the lightning, everyone in the cheap seats sought shelter under the grandstand and watched in silence. It was so loud the ground shook. These folks were no doubt more familiar with tornados than I, and it was revealed in the faces of fear around me. It never occurred to me to run out and challenge the elements to a fight because people were being frightened when all they wanted to do was continue betting on the dogs. I guess most sane folks realize when all hope of resistance is vain, no matter how brave we think we are.

But I was panicked in this moment. Fighting was the last thing on my mind, running was the first thing. I was thinking survival, and the most I could muster was what seemed to me a very feeble cry for help. I was afraid I was the only one who could hear it, or maybe I was only dreaming that I said anything at all. Even my voice had failed me.

But my cry was met with a thunderous rumble that shook the trees and put birds to flight. Then, everything was momentarily silent and two winged giants appeared next to me. The flashing sword stopped turning and retreated back to its starting place. The giants picked me up by the arms, gently lifted me off the ground and carried me into the forest.

As I was carried across the borderland from the wilderness, the environment changed dramatically. The bright sun was filtered by all of the trees and there was a refreshing coolness instead of the dry heat. The winged giants put me down in a meadow full of flowers. The scent was sweet and intoxicating. I was aware that I was in a safe place. Being me, I was arrogantly confident that I was ready for whatever was going to happen next.

It was so quiet that it seemed like there was an absence of life. The silence was broken by the sound of something moving nearby. Fear gripped me as I anticipated what I was going to see next. I intently stared in the direction of the sounds, looking for something while at the same time afraid to see it.

Before I saw anything, a brilliant light broke through the thick growth of greenery that surrounded the meadow. It was like the flash-bang grenades that SWAT uses to disorient suspects. The light blinded me and I fell forward trying to shelter my eyes with the ground. Even in this position, I couldn't shut out the brightness.

Then a deep voice spoke, "Duke, I heard your cry for help. It's okay to look. I will tone down the light."

I cautiously peeked up. As my eyes adjusted, I saw a being unlike anything I had ever seen or imagined. It was huge and had the appearance of a masculine figure. I was reminded of a hologram as the being's appearance seemed to change as I moved my head to get a better look. The only word I could think of was majestic, so powerful that being in his presence left me with no strength. I couldn't even hold my head up. It sort of flopped forward on its own and I thought, "This must be what a boneless chicken feels like."

He spoke again, but this time his voice was softer, "Come on Duke, try again. I will help you." When I peeked up this time, he was looking at my face and his appearance was warm and smiling. I had the feeling that he could see right through me. Then something unbelievable happened that took away my fear. He reached down and lifted my face with his hands, so that we were making eye contact. I felt the power in his touch, and yet he was so gentle that I was not afraid of him ripping my head off.

He asked me what I thought I was doing in his garden. I tried to gather my thoughts. I stuttered an apology and clumsily told him I was LAPD. "The folks who brought me here seem to think I can help them with the death of that young man outside," I nervously continued, "I'm finding it hard to breathe in your presence."

He softly replied, "Duke, you have nothing to fear. When you called on me in church, I heard you. You are safe with me. I would never have allowed you into my garden had you not asked me for deliverance. Now, what do you think you're doing in my garden?"

"There are so many things," I was trying to gather my thoughts, "Did I die when I got shot and did Jaden do it?"

"Are you injured?" He asked.

"I think I was shot in the back of the head."
"Have you checked to see how badly you were wounded?"

"No, sir, to tell you the truth, I'm afraid to know," I responded.

"Check it out, Duke."

I slowly reached for the back of my head. I wasn't kidding about not wanting to know. I felt all right, but didn't know if I was bleeding, or how bad my wounds might be. I touched the back of my head, feeling what I was sure was a crusty piece of bone. "My skull," I said aloud. Yet, it didn't hurt to touch it, so I continued to probe with my fingers. I felt a soft, sticky substance that had to be my brains. I pulled my hand away. "I'm dead, aren't I?" I asked the Lord.

"You don't look dead to me," he answered."

"I told you I didn't want to know. Jaden blew my brains out, didn't he? Is there anything you can do?"

He laughed, "I guess it depends on what you believe about me when you say, 'If there's anything I can do.' Let me help you. Why don't you smell your fingers?" he instructed.

A strange suggestion, but I pulled my hand to my nose. It reeked so bad I jerked my head back. "This smells like dog poop," I said. He smiled, "I think you'll be all right once you clean yourself. Why don't you use the stream over there to wash?" I had seen this stream from the top of the hill. Up close it looked so clear that the water was invisible.

After I rinsed off my hands and head, I turned back toward Him, "Can I ask a question from my bible reading?"

His voice was firmer now and his appearance flashed the look of a lion, "You can't stay here, Duke. I won't tell you anything that is not written in my word. I have provided everything that is adequate for mankind to know in the scriptures. I am pleased at how you have turned there to see what I have to say, and I trust you to find your answers there."

I was fairly certain that I was dreaming, so I took a chance of pushing it, "But sir, won't you please tell me a couple of things? Will I see my mom and dad in heaven? You know I never got to love them before they died."
"That's not in my word. You'll have to wait to find out. What's the other question?"

"How painful was the crucifixion?"

His appearance took on a look of sorrow as he spoke. "You know that my word reveals I hated the cross and all that came with it. That was the greatest physical pain that will ever be endured on earth, because mankind cannot bear up under the amount of pain that I suffered. There is another pain that is equivalent, something more personal. For mankind, this personal pain takes away the heart. It is being stabbed in the back by one who should love you. That never ends for me.

"I never intended for anyone to suffer. I created this environment for mankind in the garden where life would work, no one would die, and true love would be the experience of everyone. That love would have always been faithful. I believe those are the words of your Marines, right?"

"Semper fidelis?" I guessed.

"Ah, always faithful, how sweet the sound; a dependent faithfulness on me that would never be violated. So when Adam committed the crime against me, by not fighting for me or for his wife, the change went from semper fidelis to semper perfidious, always treacherous!" There was the lion appearance again. "That is why faithfulness and loyalty are emphasized so strongly in my word, they are what I desire and value.

" But people ignore what I desire, and blame me now that life doesn't work anymore. Even the day I endured the cross, the experience my word says I despised, your Christian culture refers to as a good day."

"You mean Good Friday?"

"Yes, Duke. A constant reminder of how narcissistic the church has become, as if people weren't self-centered enough they are taught that if it turned out good for them, they can forget what it meant for me.

"Last thing, Duke, you have seen in my word that fear trumps everything else in the hearts of mankind. Your dad was not a warrior, he was a man who was afraid, and he covered his fear by not letting anyone get close enough to see it. He wanted to be loved, but became love's executioner by his failure to come to me to see how true love works. You have done the same by covering up your fear of being a coward by becoming cocky and arrogant. That has to change. You will be broken by your own sinfulness, until you learn to hate it. Pay attention to the strength that you dismissed as a young man. When your mother took her dying breath, she gave something of herself. She reached up and touched the check of her nurse, giving her a smile and thanking her for her care."

Wow, I remembered being told that story by a young and pretty nurse who couldn't stop crying as she told me, just as I was having a hard time stopping now. His countenance shifted again, and I saw tears in his eyes and a soft, feminine appearance. "You must leave now."

He gave a signal that brought the winged creatures back. They picked me up, but he had them set me back down. I wasn't sure what to expect as he approached me. He now appeared masculine and strong. He grabbed me. I had never been hugged by a man before, this was one I could never forget even if it was a dream. As he held me, he whispered in my ear, "Never forget the first crime scene."

Then I was air lifted out of the garden and placed down in the wilderness. The ground was hard; the heat was draining, as I started the ascent back up the hill to where I had left Adam and Eve. My mind raced as I tried to remember the Lord's words, and put them together with what I had been reading in the scriptures. Suddenly, it was as if he turned on a light in my heart, and I remembered, "You gave knowledge to Adam when you warned him not to eat the forbidden fruit. You told him it would cause death. But how would Adam know what death meant, when he had never experienced it?"

My heart ached as I remembered how he and Eve groaned over the death of their son. Now they knew...now they knew! Life experience helped them understand what the Lord had told them, and it was too much for them to bear! Now Adam knew he was responsible for destroying everything they wanted for their children. "That's why they sit at the top of the hill, looking at the garden. They never knew what they really wanted until they had lost it! And if you don't know what you want, you won't fight for anything."

I told myself I had to start paying attention to the things I wanted, so I could trust them to God and not ignore them. "Then they already have the answer to what happened to Abel. How terrible to know his brother killed him," I told myself, "but why did he tell me to always remember that first crime scene?"

When I reached the top of the hill, no one was there. I wanted to find Adam. I was winded, so I sat on one of the carefully placed rocks and looked down at the garden.

My heart stopped. I was crushed. I collapsed, face down, weeping so hard I couldn't catch a breath. "Lord, I'm such a fool that I missed what you were telling me. I thought the murder of Abel was the first crime scene." I looked again at the garden. It had yellow crime scene tape around it now, as far as I could see.

"Now I know," I sobbed, "you were the first victim of the first crime: betrayal." I caught my breath and shouted as loud as I could, "Betrayal!" I remembered painful moments when I had been betrayed. "Lord, I want vengeance when I'm betrayed, yet you didn't waiver or change your purpose to teach us true love. What you get in return is us treating you as if you are too big or too impersonal to be hurt. You are the forgotten victim in all of our crimes, a man of sorrows, acquainted with grief." It took me a while before I could breathe again. When I did, I thanked him over and over for putting up with me for as long as he had.

VIII. _LIGHT_

The path of the righteous is like the light of dawn that shines brighter and brighter until the full day. The way of the wicked is like darkness. They do not know over what they stumble. (Proverbs 4:18-19)

The light was blinding me again. Even though my eyes were closed, the light was piercing and painful. I reached toward it and my hand hit something hard.

"Sergeant, are you all right?"

I carefully opened my eyes and tried to adjust. The shiny helmet of the sheriff's deputy came into view. "Where am I?" I was lying on my back looking up.

The deputy was kneeling over me. "You're at the bottom of the hill, sir. It looks like you took a nasty fall. The detectives sent me up here when they got a call from a resident saying they heard what sounded like a gunshot. The detectives asked me to investigate and told me that you had come up here to do an interview. The neighbor across the street told me the gunshot came from this area, so I started searching the hillside and found you here. Are you hurt? Do you want me to call an ambulance?"

I asked him to give me a few minutes to get my bearings. I tried to take an inventory to see where I felt pain. I looked down and still had my legs, although my levis were covered with dirt and debris. I could move my arms. The back of my head hurt. I started to feel my head and then I remembered something. "My head really hurts. Would you check the back of my head to see if I'm OK?" I asked the young deputy. He removed the glove from his right hand and carefully felt the back of my head. "This is bad, sir, I'm calling an ambulance. You're worse than you realize. Please lie still and don't try to move."

I told him it felt like he pulled off part of my skull and asked him to check his hand. As he pulled it out from under my head, I saw his eyes get big. "What the hell?" he blurted as he shined his light on his hand and saw that it was full of dog poop. He hurriedly wiped his hand on some brush nearby. "I've got to go to my car and get something to clean my hand," he said as he started to walk away. I asked him to leave his light and I used it to track my fall down the hill. Not too far from where I stopped, I saw what must have been a dump taken by a giant pit bull. There were streakers going through it, so I checked my clothes. Clean. I was amazed to imagine that I must have come through the poop standing on my head. By then I was laughing out loud, sure the deputy would think I was loopy from the fall. I looked up through the trees and smiled, knowing the Lord was reminding me that I'd had a head full of poop my entire adult life.

The deputy returned and as I steadied myself on my feet, his light illuminated an area nearby and he asked, "Is this yours?" In the dirt, near where I had been lying was a handgun. I could see it wasn't mine and I reached for my waistband. My levi jacket had protected my upper body and my .45 auto was still tucked where it should be. I picked up the handgun from the ground, and I looked up the hillside. There was a trail showing I had fallen about 100 yards. "My training worked," I whispered to the Lord, "Jaden must be right handed."

Once on my feet, I started to walk toward the street with the deputy at my side. I sensed he was there to catch me, anticipating that I was not going to make it on my own. I asked him not to touch me with his poopy hand. He laughed because I still had my hair matted with the smelly stuff.

Once we reached the street, I saw my car and told him I was going to drive to the sheriff's station to check in with the detectives. I thanked him for going out of his way to find and help me. Before I left, he asked me if I had heard a gunshot. I didn't want to answer before I decided how I was going to handle my situation, so I told him I heard nothing before I slipped and fell down the hill. Later, I would write him a commendation for his attention to duty.

• • • • •

It was only a short drive to the station. I went inside and held my head under the bathroom faucet, then I returned to the car. I had parked the car in a dark corner of the parking lot. I closed my eyes and leaned on the steering wheel, taking a few more minutes to try to clear my head.

My time in the garden was still fresh in my mind and seemed graphically real, yet I wondered if I had just been hallucinating. Still I prayed, asking the Lord to help me remember the dream and thanking him for saving my butt once again and apologizing for all the other times he had bailed me out and I had ignored it.

That prayer caused me to consider what I was going to do next. Often in my efforts to prove myself, I had stumbled into situations that could have ruined my career or at least embarrassed me and ruined my reputation. I realized I was in that situation now. "What are my options?" I mused. If I report what happened, not only will I be criticized for going out by myself, my judgment will be questioned for falling into an obvious trap. That would mean being pulled off this case and it could have a detrimental effect on my supervisors for not managing me more closely.

I decided I would tell no one what had happened. I could not disclose that I had found the weapon that had been used in the attack, so I left the handgun under the car seat and entered the sheriff's station.

I thanked the detective who dispatched the deputy to look for me and assured him that I was fine and had fallen down the hillside while checking the area around Jaden's house. I told him that I hadn't gotten an answer when I went to the door, and was snooping around when I slipped and fell. Then I used one of the phones in the station and dialed Jaden's number. Hannah answered. "I know Jaden is there. What you assholes did tonight was personal. I want you to know I'm coming after you and I will take you down." I hung up without waiting for a response.

● ● ● ● ●

In order to clear my head some more, I drove to the donut shop where the owner had gotten to know me. He was closed and busy making donuts for the next day, but he unlocked when he saw it was me. Hot coffee was already brewing and I had plenty of fresh donuts to choose from. I brought the gun inside to look at it more closely. It was a

Spanish made Llama 9 mm automatic, blue steel with brown handles. I saw that the slide was partially jammed open and I was unable to budge it. When I left the donut shop, I stuffed it back beneath the seat making a mental memo to take it to one of my gun friends tomorrow. That caused me to remember I already had a long list of things to do for the coming day.

I arrived before sun-up and my wife wasn't waiting this morning. That was a good thing because I didn't want to try to answer any questions about how I looked. I jumped in the shower, which woke her up, but by the time she saw me I was clean. I found some ibuprofen and swallowed a few before I hit the sack. The throbbing in my head continued but nothing could keep me from falling asleep this morning.

My wife awakened me at noon to see if I was taking the day off. I called the office to let them know I had worked late and then headed for the academy. I had a friend there who worked the range. I told him I had found the small automatic and asked him why it was jammed. He put me to shame with the ease in which he took it apart. He pulled a slug from the barrel. "Whoever tried to fire this thing was using some really old ammo. They don't even make these bullets anymore," he informed me.

"Does that mean the gun could fire, but without enough force for the bullet to strike it's intended target?" I asked. "Right, the sound could be the same, but the gun powder in this bullet was so old that the slug just lodged in the barrel and jammed the gun. If the shooter intended on hitting someone, that person would be one lucky son of a bitch who probably had to run home to change his shorts," he answered. We ran gun records and found no record on the gun.

I left the academy thinking about how crazy Jaden was and wondering how I could be smarter in working my case. I figured it would be a good idea to let someone know what had happened in case Jaden tried to set me up again. I headed to see my new friend Dave at DEA. In trying to think about what Jaden would expect me to do, I figured he'd be looking over his shoulder for me everywhere he went. Maybe it was a good time for me to lay low for a few days.

Dave met me for lunch in Westwood. He was really concerned to hear what Jaden had done, but wasn't surprised. This is the stuff of urban legends, but something rarely encountered in police work. He told me I could trust him to keep the info between us and that he had some good informants who could work Jaden. His main guy was George from Malibu who knew both Max and Jaden. George was busted in a sting operation and had attempted to buy dope from Dave. Dave had begun to work him and George had turned some good information, including the attempted sale of heroin where Max, Barry and Carl were busted. He told me he would arrange a meeting between me and George. We then went to his office to see what we could find in the federal records systems.

● ● ● ● ●

Jaden had come to the attention of law enforcement when he was drafted into the Army during Viet Nam. His dad was career military. Jaden became a radical trouble maker and fell in with the anti-war crowd. While stationed at Fort Dix, he was convicted of engaging in a conspiracy to disrupt the base and sentenced to do time at Leavenworth. It was during his time in the Army that he had married Karen and they later had one son. Dave provided me with contact information for Karen. She lived in Malibu. I knew I could get more information on her from Krissy. While in prison, Jaden met Carl and upon his release he moved to the west coast.

He served all of his time and was released without parole; in the vernacular he did not have a tail.

Hannah was foreign born, entering the country as a Dutch citizen. Her status in this country was uncertain, especially since she had been arrested in Los Angeles. Dave made a call to a friend of his at INS. His friend took the info we had on Hannah and made an appointment with us, telling us he would do some research before our meeting.

I next went to West Valley detectives to find out more about the car they had recovered. The car had been left in a residential area along Mulholland Drive a little more than five miles east of where Max had been buried. A resident called for a patrol car to check it out and it was determined that the car had been reported stolen by Diana Black. The lab had thoroughly searched the car, a 1968 Cadillac, and the area around the car. Some partial fingerprints had been lifted from the windows. The car had then been impounded and the West Valley detectives had put a hold on it so no one could release it except me.

I drove to the area where the car was found just to look around and talk to some of the neighbors. No one had seen who parked the car, nor had they seen anyone around since the car was left. The man who had called the police had written down the time when he first saw the car parked. It was at 1:30pm on the day Max's body had been discovered.

I drove to the lab at Van Nuys Division to look at the property that was removed from the car. Nothing significant was found in the interior or the trunk, only some porn magazines and a copy of the LA Free Press. I noticed the newspaper had been opened to the personals and that there was a circle drawn around an ad for a swinger's party. I made a Xerox copy of the page and gave the lab a list of suspects to compare with the fingerprints they had lifted from the car.

The stolen report showed Diana's address in an area south of LAX. I called Krissy to see if she knew Diana. "She's Max's ex-girl friend. They lived together while Max was working a club in Fresno a couple of years ago. Max told me it was over between them."

I called the number Diana had given on the police report and spoke with a man named Farley. He said Diana had left for work and would be home around midnight. I asked him where she worked and he asked me not to bother her there. She was a topless dancer and could easily get fired. Carl said Diana was his girlfriend, so I told him I would be at the house to talk to him before midnight and then wait for Diana to get home. He agreed and told me he would call Diana to make sure she came straight home from work. I figured they would want to cooperate to get the car back.

I tried calling the number from the swinger's ad but got no answer. I called the Free Press, a paper not exactly known for cooperating with law enforcement. After being told the identity of the person who placed the ad was confidential information, I reasoned with them by telling them I was on my way to pick up the information. "If you don't have it ready, I will be returning with a search warrant and then you get to watch me search your offices for it."

The information was waiting when I arrived at their offices in Hollywood. The ad had been placed by a man named Timmy. The paper said the ad was soliciting singles and couples to join a service that provided dating opportunities. The ad also offered astrology readings for a fee. I got Timmy's phone number from the paper. When I called, the man who answered said Timmy had left town to meet with his warlock who lived at Moss Landing. It seemed like too weird a story to be made up on the moment, and I hung up without identifying myself. I had to look up Moss Landing. It was on the coast, a little south of the bay area. Then I called Krissy to ask her what a warlock was. She told me it is a male witch and told me if I wanted to know more she could put me in touch with a weird friend of Jaden's named Timmy.

• • • • •

I arrived at Diana's around 11pm. The house was in a rundown neighborhood. Farley was a biker who volunteered that he'd been busted for using drugs. He had been living with Diana for a few weeks and had met Max in July when he showed up at Diana's work. Farley said Diana told him about her relationship with Max. He said the three of them got along as friends.

After Max was arrested, he had told Farley about being afraid of Jaden, whom Farley did not know. Max told him Jaden was a big time dealer with a lot of connections. Max told Farley that Barry had ratted them out but that Jaden was suspicious of Max. "Max said the feds had offered him a deal if he wanted to work off his case, but he told me he refused."

"He would show up and hang out a couple of times a week after his arrest. The last time I saw him was on a Friday in September. I was driving Diana's car and Max asked me to meet him at a bar in Torrance at 6pm. We had one drink and then he asked me to drive him to Diana's. In the car, he told me that he had talked to Jaden on the phone that day and Jaden ordered him to meet some guys at a place in the valley that night. Jaden told him he was going to have the other two guys in the arrest killed so that no one could snitch off Jaden's operation. Max said he believed Jaden because Barry was already known as a rat and Carl was Jaden's courier for his Mexican connection. Jaden felt Carl knew too much and Jaden was pissed at Carl for going on the deal with him."

Farley continued to recall his conversation, "Max said the hit wasn't going down that night, but he wanted to go to the meeting to find out when and where it would take place. He said that way he could be sure to have an alibi when it happened. He made me promise not to tell Diana. Diana went to work at nine that night. Max told her he had a meeting at eleven and he needed her car. He dropped her and me off at her club and left in her Cady. When he didn't bring the car back I told Diana what he had told me. We called everyone we could think of that weekend, but nobody had seen Max. We borrowed a car and drove around Hollywood and the valley looking for Diana's car. Finally, by Monday we were scared that something had happened to Max and Diana reported the car stolen."

Diana arrived home as Farley and I were talking. She put on some coffee and sat down to talk. She was a nice looking young woman, someone you would take for a school teacher if you saw her on the street. I asked Farley to leave us alone for a few minutes. I wanted to make sure I got her story without any influence from him. She told me the same story in the same detail. She said she had met Max in Fresno in 1972. She was working there when he got a regular gig with his band. He was a great entertainer and made good money. She never saw him use dope, but said he always carried a gun. They moved in together for a couple of months in 1973 before breaking up. He showed up at her work recently. He told her about trying to commit suicide after his arrest for selling dope. She had been out of touch with Max from the time they broke up until he came to her work in July. She gave me the name and number of the guy she lived with after she broke up with Max, saying he would verify her story. She said it wouldn't be hard for Max to find her since they had many common friends who knew her whereabouts. "Even his mom knew how to reach me." She had struck up a phone friendship with Rose when she was living with Max and had stayed in touch with her. "The last time I saw him was on a Friday evening. He was wearing a white jacket and red and white plaid pants. He didn't have a gun that I could see. He took my key ring with all of my keys." Diana got her personal phone book and gave me the names and numbers of people she said knew Max, some were local, some were in Fresno.

It was early in the morning hours again and I had over an hour's drive home. I had arranged to meet Dave the next morning at ten at the downtown offices of the Immigration and Naturalization Service. The car hit some really high speeds that night. I always marveled at people who complained about the police driving too fast. If they needed help, I wondered how many would demand that we obey all the traffic laws.

IX. *IMMIGRATION*

For why should you, my son, be exhilarated with an adulteress and embrace the bosom of a foreigner? (Proverbs 5:20)

The federal building in downtown Los Angeles is less than a block from LAPD headquarters, known as Parker Center and often referred to as "the glass house". All of the citywide specialized detective divisions are housed on the third floor. Parking in the civic center is nearly impossible, so I arranged for Dave to park in the police parking lot. He met me in my office and we walked to the INS offices in the federal building. I was reminded once more, how it is the personal relationships that get the work accomplished. Dave introduced me to his friend, Bob, an INS agent. Like me, Dave and Bob had been working at their specialties for years and knew what worked and what didn't, inside their agencies. Bob had a file on Hannah that he had already reviewed. She had entered the country by acquiring a green card, probably with the influence of her father, an ambassador for the Netherlands. Bob had found a situation in her status that stirred up interest for me and Dave. Her status carried a stipulation that allowed for her stay to be revoked should she be convicted of a felony while in the U.S. All three of us were aware that she had pled out to possession of heroin charges, a felony, some two years prior. I asked Bob if his agency is notified upon felony convictions and he said that such notifications quite often never make it to INS. "It would require someone in the legal system to take the initiative," he said, "and as with most cases like this, no one even inquires as to a defendant's citizenship status. The good news in this case, is that now I know."

We asked Bob what he could do to help us, and he asked me if I could get more information on Hannah's conviction. From the records, we could see that she did not serve any jail time, and that she was still on formal probation.

Dave and I returned to my office. We identified Hannah's probation officer with a phone call to probation department records. The P/O was named Betty and she was assigned to the Metro office not far from Parker Center. I reached Betty on the phone and tried to arrange an appointment. She was evasive, so I tried to emphasize the importance of a meeting. She claimed to be too busy for a meeting and insisted on knowing the name of the probationer I wanted to see her about. I identified Hannah to her and she put me on hold. She returned to say she had checked Hannah's file and that she was currently shooting a movie in Las Vegas. I asked why she believed that to be true, and she said, "Her husband called and told me. He's cancelled most of her appearances because she's having a successful acting career. It's not my job to interfere with rehabilitation."

I asked Betty if that meant she had not been testing Hannah for drug use as required by the court that sentenced her, and what Hannah's husband's name was. With a defensive and irritated tone in her voice she said, "Look, I do the best I can with more people to watch than is humanly possible. I'm stuck when Jaden calls, that's her husband, Jaden. He either cancels or appears with her. I've never seen Hannah when Jaden wasn't present and because she is doing so well, I have given her permission to travel."

I then informed Betty that Jaden was himself a hype and the supplier of Hannah's heroin and that she daily shoots up with him. I also told her that she was not making movies. "If you would like to go with me," I said, "I'll take you to where she is living right now and you can ask her yourself."

Betty told me if I could document my claims, that she would file a desertion order, but made it clear that she didn't believe I knew as much about Hannah as I thought I did. A desertion order would revoke Hannah's probation. Dave called Bob and asked what he could do if Hannah's probation was violated and Bob said he would file the paperwork to begin deportation proceedings. When Dave told me this, I called Bob back and asked him if we arranged for Hannah to be placed in custody for probation violation, if he could place a hold on her that would keep her in custody. He said he could arrange for that to happen. I was getting excited.

I made copies of the necessary paperwork for Betty and dropped them at her office. I insisted on seeing her so that I could tell her Hannah was involved in a murder investigation and that I expected her to keep confidential everything we had discussed. I told Betty that if Hannah got wind of the possibility of her probation being revoked, she would likely flee. Betty looked just the way she sounded on the phone, angry, and only nodded without saying anything. I told her I would follow up to find out when Hannah could be arrested.

• • • • •

I took Dave to lunch at the academy. The police academy is a historic and interesting place to visit, even for other law enforcement officers. Tucked into the hills of Chavez Ravine, it's less than a ten minute drive from Parker Center. It had been used as a firing range for the 1932 Olympics, before any of the buildings were there. Driving to the academy from downtown requires going through Chavez Ravine, a once small community of Mexicans who had lived there since the 1800's. The neighborhood had been self-sufficient with the residents even growing their own crops. By the 1950's, the country had bought into the idea of living under big government, and the inevitable result of bureaucracy led to the city viewing the beautiful open spaces of Chavez Ravine, located so close to the civic center, as a cash cow. Through the abuse of eminent domain laws, the folks living in Chavez Ravine had their property taken under the guise of the public good. A failed attempt at building public housing in the area set the stage for the eventual building of Dodger Stadium.

The academy itself contains many artifacts of LAPD history, a café open to the public and private facilities just for LAPD, such as a gym, swimming pool, basketball courts, and a rock garden with waterfalls and pools. I had married my wife in the rock garden.

I always walked my guests down what I called the trophy hallway, where I could point to the plaques that bore the names of my friends, Art and my captain, for their accomplishments in basketball.

88

After lunch, I called Hannah's P/O to see if she had violated Hannah's probation. She told me she had. I asked her when Hannah was scheduled for her next visit. She said it was due in a couple of weeks and that she would try to contact Hannah to tell her it was a mandatory appearance. I asked her if I could assist with the arrest and Betty said, "Absolutely not!" After hanging up, I pondered showing up at the probation office anyway, and then thought better of it.

The holidays were approaching and I was determined to give more of my time and attention to my family and to the Lord. We had settled into a routine of attending church and were developing some good friendships with normal people and I sensed my family was starting to feel safer with me.

The next couple of weeks were less hectic. I had time to continue networking by staying in touch with Dave and Bob. I also contacted my friend, Bob, at Rampart Detectives to check on the progress of the Charles Smith murder. He sounded disappointed, telling me he got stuck assigning the case to one of his laziest detectives and that nothing had been developed. He threw in a positive note by saying his guys told him they might have an informant who could break the case.

• • • • •

On the date of Hannah's scheduled appearance with her P/O, I made sure to make myself available. Dave called me that morning to tell me that he too, had requested to be present at Hannah's arrest, telling Betty that the DEA had worked the case that had been filed against her. He had been rebuffed not only by her, but by her supervisor. "They told me it would be too dangerous if I was there." The day passed without either of us being called.

That evening, I couldn't resist driving past Jaden's residence. There was no activity to indicate anyone was home. I worried that Jaden and Hannah had gotten wind of the probation violation and had split. The next morning I placed a call to Betty. She told me

Hannah had been arrested and booked at the Sybil Brand Institute for Women.

SBI was a minimum security jail located in City Terrace, on the east side of downtown Los Angeles. I contacted Dave and Bob to give them the news and to let them know that I was going to attempt to interview Hannah. I asked Bob to move ahead with deportation and he said he was way ahead of me.

I had Hannah pulled to an interrogation room. She was not surprised to see me and had a fairly decent attitude. She put me on notice that she knew nothing about Jaden or his business that would help me. She said he was so broke and had no credit, that he had rented the house in the name of a financially solvent friend, Hal. She leaked something I might be able to use by telling me that Jaden's wife, Karen, was putting a lot of pressure on him for a divorce and that she was driving Jaden crazy with her financial demands. "He has to hide a lot from her," Hannah revealed. I hadn't yet spoken to Karen, but I realized that I needed to see her soon.

I asked her to tell me about Max, and she said, "Jaden and I liked him a lot. I didn't know much about him. You can find out more by talking to Krissy and Sugar. They both lived with him. Max would stop by every once in a while to see Jaden. I never knew him to use dope. Max would say he was staying in Malibu. He told Jaden he was spying on Karen for him."

I asked Hannah if she used narcotics and she denied it. I then took hold of her left hand and pulled it toward me, exposing her inner arm. Fresh needle marks could be seen. She got upset at this and said, "So we use heroin, you already know that. I'm definitely not hooked. I shot up three times yesterday before I saw my P/O. She told me you had snitched me off. She probably gave you some bullshit story about not testing me because I was out of town doing movies. Truth is, she hasn't tested me for months because Jaden was paying her not to."

I asked if she had ever seen Jaden hurt anybody, baiting her by asking if he is as weak as he appears, "I've heard from reliable sources that he's gay," I added. She became defensive, "He goes crazy when he gets mad. His wife told me once that she left him because he was beating her and their son. I pissed him off once and he grabbed an axe and chased me through the house swinging at me. The marks are still on the upstairs walls and doors."

I asked her if she had ever killed anyone or if she was there when Max was murdered. "Not me. I have to admit that Jaden acted strange after I saw Max for the last time. He came by the house during the week that he disappeared to talk to Jaden. After that week, I never saw him again and Jaden never mentioned his name. I wanted to ask Jaden about what happened, but his look told me not to ask."

I told her I didn't like her, and that I would keep my word to pay her back for her part in trying to ambush me. She didn't deny it. She said, "I'm afraid of Jaden. I love him and stay with him because he takes care of me. I told him that I didn't want to do that, and that he should cooperate with you if he didn't kill Max. He wouldn't do it because he hates you."

She then acted confident that I couldn't do anything to her. "Jaden and I got married in Vegas. I know that makes him a bigamist, but who cares about that? I can never be forced to testify against him," she said with a cocky smile.

Hannah did not know about the hold that INS had placed on her which would keep her in custody. I had the pleasure of looking her in the eyes and telling her. I saw fire inside, as she bit her lip to keep from attacking me. When I smiled, it was too much for her and she blurted out, "There's nothing you can do to me. My dad is an ambassador, my mom has remarried a federal judge, and I'm close to a senator, very close. Give it your best shot. You'll get your ass kicked!" And with that she got up and called for a guard to take her back to her cell.

Bob called me the next day to tell me that Hannah's probation hold had been removed and she had bailed out of jail by posting a bond with the INS. He was obviously upset when he told me he didn't know how it happened. Her hearing was to take place between Thanksgiving and Christmas.

X. *KAREN*

How long, O simple-minded ones, will you love naiveté? (Proverbs 1:22)

Of all the risky things that I found myself doing because I didn't have a partner, I knew the most dangerous one was meeting with female informants. First, informants were not trustworthy and could turn on you without warning; second, should a female allege that anything sexual happened, I would find myself on the defense. That was not a good thing to imagine, but whenever the risk seemed worth it to break a case, I usually took it. Trying to figure safe-guards was difficult as these meetings were almost always clandestine. If the woman decided to help, as in the case of Krissy, the risk then shifted to her. Meeting in secret was one way to protect informants. I also kept my lieutenant informed whenever I could do so without shifting the risk upon him in case something went wrong.

When it was time to contact Jaden's wife, Karen, I initially tried to get her to meet me in a secluded public place, a restaurant in Malibu where no one would know who I was even if someone recognized her. Although Karen sounded eager to talk to me, she insisted that I come to her home. I reluctantly agreed.

Karen was an attractive girl, petite with dark hair and eyes. She greeted me and took me into the kitchen of the home that she and Jaden owned. The house was clean and nicely furnished, but it would be considered modest by the standard of homes in Malibu.

Karen was rather talkative, controlling the conversation and steering it to small talk. As I feared, she had taken my agreement to come to her home as more than a business meeting. She prepared a margarita for both of us and then started tending to a dinner she was cooking. I tried to explain that I couldn't stay, but my excuse was so lame that it bothered even me, and she refused to hear me.

She talked about herself and Jaden as if telling me a soap opera. It seemed so full of fluff, that I wondered if I had wasted my time coming to see her. She was overtly naïve. Even when Jaden was arrested at Fort Dix, she told the story as if it were a casual event, common to all newlyweds.

It wasn't until after the meal that she started to get serious. Her demeanor changed from cute and frivolous to being frightened. "Jaden left home last month and didn't come back. He called after a few days to tell me he was staying away to decide if he was going to divorce me. I went to Atlanta where I had a successful modeling career and stayed with friends. After a month of not hearing from him, I flew back and located him at the Beverly Hills Hotel. I went to his room and Hannah answered the door. Jaden told me to get lost.

"I got an attorney and checked our bank accounts. We had several hundred thousand dollars when I left, and Jaden had zeroed out all of our accounts. We had opened an office for a business we called Budd Productions."

I asked Karen about the source of the money and if Budd was a legitimate business or a front. Jaden had told her he made the money by investing with high-rollers in the entertainment business and that's why he wanted to open his own production company. She said the name had something to do with Jaden's Buddhist beliefs.

Karen continued, "When I went to the Budd office, I was surprised to find Jaden there. It looked like he was moving things out. When he saw me coming off the elevator, he hit me so hard it knocked me down and then he started kicking me. He had beaten me often, even slapping me in public. I knew he was crazy, so whenever he got violent I always started screaming. If I remained quiet, I was sure he would keep going until he killed me."

I asked her about Jaden's jail time. "When he got in trouble with the Army, his parents paid for the legal battle. They live in Florida. I met Jaden in New York where I was doing some acting.

I didn't care about politics, so when he told me he was a pacifist it really didn't mean anything. After I met him, the FBI picked us up and questioned me about Jaden being a spy. We were married in a Buddhist ceremony. He traveled around making anti-war speeches. When Jane Fonda came to Fort Dix to support us, we stayed with her for several days. Later, I realized all his liberal friends were idiots. When he was arrested none of them offered to help us so I went to a conservative senator from my home state. He took my call and got bail set for Jaden.

"Anyway, he was convicted and served four years. When he got out we moved to New York. We lived there until a couple of years ago when we moved here. I don't know what Jaden did in New York. He was very secretive. I met Carl Mobley there. Jaden told me he had met Carl in prison and that he was going to bring him with us to California to open the business. I could tell Carl was using heroin and asked Jaden not to bring him. Jaden said they were partners and if anyone ever asked me about him and I talked, that he or Carl would kill me. Carl brought his girlfriend, a black girl named Dorothy, with him. She took whatever she wanted of my clothes and jewelry. There was nothing I could say or Jaden would hurt me."

About this time, I was beginning to believe Karen, although her behavior now was contradictory to the illusion of life she had presented when we began. I knew she and Jaden had a son so I asked her where the boy was. She broke down in tears.

"Jaden took him last week. He called to tell me that the police were hounding him and might try to find me. He said if I talked to the police, he would kill our son."

I waited until she calmed down and asked her what she intended to do next. She said she had already seen two attorneys about filing a divorce and seeing what they could do to keep Jaden from their son. She said both attorneys had contacted Jaden and then both had withdrawn from representing her. She gave me their names.

Karen said she didn't know Max very well. "He was a friend of Jaden's." She expressed shock when I told her Max had been murdered, saying she did not know. "When I came back from Atlanta, Max phoned me to say that Jaden was in love with Hannah. He was very considerate and said Jaden was treating me unfairly. He said something about Jaden making a mess of business because of Hannah. The next day, Jaden called me and I told him what Max had said. Jaden said if Max was talking to me, he was going to bash his head in."

I told Karen I would check with her attorneys to see if there was something that could be done to get her son back. When I started to stand, she pushed me back and tried to kiss me. She really seemed disturbed, and I had to be forceful in getting her to let me go. I tried to let her know that I cared about her welfare, and that it was dangerous for her to meet with me. I knew I might want her as a witness some day, so I tried to let her know that she was attractive, but that this was a matter of business. I left thanking the Lord for protecting me and assured him I'd never meet Karen in private again.

● ● ● ● ●

The first attorney Karen had contacted agreed to talk to me, but only if I promised it was off the record. He said he had contacted Jaden after Karen retained him. When he stated his business, Jaden hung up on him. Within a short time, Jaden appeared at his office with a big black guy and told him if he represented Karen, he would have an accident and both of his legs would be broken. He immediately withdrew from the case.

The second attorney Karen had contacted, said when he first contacted Jaden, he had been threatened also and decided not to represent Karen. Then an attorney contacted him, saying he represented Jaden so he decided to stay on the case. After I told him I had interviewed Karen, he requested a meeting between the three of us. I agreed and returned later that evening. The attorney had prepared the paperwork to file for a divorce. Karen seemed more at ease, and said Jaden had brought their son back the night before. "He came with a black guy who had a gun in his belt. He told me he was trading our son, Jackie, for me moving out of the house so he could move in. He said I had to be out today, but I'm not going to do it. He said he lost his lease on the Hollywood Hills house because of you, Duke."

Her attorney confirmed her story, saying he had talked to the owner of the house in the hills. When the owner heard about the party and arrests, he went in and saw an incredible amount of damage. Floors and carpets had been ruined, statues and candelabras were missing. The owner had made a police report alleging $5,000 of malicious mischief and $11,000 of theft. He added that walls and doors had been damaged with what appeared to be knife or ax marks. "Even a piano I left in the house was permanently damaged with ax marks. Judy Garland had used the piano in one of her movies," the owner said.

I asked Karen how her son was doing. "He told me when his dad got angry, he held his head under water in the bathtub until he couldn't breathe." Karen said he had done similar things to her and added, "I saw him beat an old man senseless once when he tried to stick up for me. Jaden's really tough when it comes to beating women and children."

I was really starting to hate this bastard.

● ● ● ● ●

The next afternoon I received a call from Karen's attorney. The night before, Jaden had forced his way into the Malibu house and removed the washer, dryer and refrigerator. The attorney had called this morning telling Jaden he had prepared divorce papers for his signature. Jaden showed up at his office, grabbed the papers and tore them up. He then grabbed a file from the attorney's desk and attempted to leave with it. The attorney had fought Jaden and bloodied his nose, causing him to drop the file. "When he walked away, he was saying all of this was happening to him because of you. My advice is to be careful; I believe he is one dangerous asshole."

97

XI. *CONTRACT*

Do not be afraid of sudden fear, nor of the onslaught of the wicked when it comes. (Proverbs 3:25)

Within a day, Luis called twice to tell me that Jaden seemed to be losing control. "He can't stop talking about you," Luis said. In order to win his favor, it seems Hannah had embellished the interview into my declaration of war against Jaden, including my intention to tell everyone that he is a fag. Of course, she included herself as the victim in the deportation proceedings that were scheduled to take place before Christmas. Luis said Jaden had started telling anyone who would listen that he had challenged me to a man to man duel. "He said that when he faced you with a gun, you ran."

I had hoped for a long weekend with my family over Thanksgiving. Some of the families we had met at church invited us to share a cabin with them at Big Bear, about 100 miles east of Los Angeles in the San Bernardino Mountains. The ladies prepared a lavish Thanksgiving meal while the men played in the snow with the kids. After dinner, everyone gathered to offer thanksgiving to the Lord. It was especially meaningful for me, as I was beginning to realize how a change in my life's purpose was changing me. I was experiencing a new peace that came from the freedom of not having to prove myself in everything that I did. With time to reflect on this, I realized what a selfish man I had become.

On the Friday after Thanksgiving Day, I received a message from the local market that DHQ was trying to contact me. The message read that Luis called to say there was an emergency and he needed me to call him right away. There was no phone at our cabin, so I trekked through the snow to the market. A storm was throwing heavy snow to the ground, a beautiful sight. I took the kids on the walk with me. I wanted all the time with them that I could get.

Luis was frightened. He said he had received an anonymous call telling him that Krissy had been murdered for being my snitch and that her body had been cut into pieces and left in her apartment. This was a call I had feared getting, and I asked Luis if he had done anything to confirm the call. He said he tried to call Krissy but got no answer and he was afraid to go there by himself. I realized that was a good thing, otherwise he could become a suspect if he chanced upon a crime scene. I told him to sit tight and I would see what I could do. Although he said he couldn't identify the caller who gave him the news, he was convinced it came from Jaden.

The kids were afraid I was going to have to leave the cabin to go back to work. I had left all of my contact information at the cabin so we had some fun racing back. I retrieved Krissy's address and phone number and set off for the pay phone. I tried calling her but got no answer. I called DHQ and asked them to have the dispatcher send a patrol car to Krissy's address and to use caution, as it may be a crime scene. I asked to be called at the market so I would know what they found.

The boys had made the second trip with me, so I sent them back to the cabin to tell my wife and daughter that I was waiting at the market for a call. The market served coffee and donuts, so I told the boys to come back and they could help me do some police work by eating donuts with me.

I thanked the Lord for the moment, as I watched my three guys dressed in coats and boots, waddling through the snow for the cabin. There was seven years between the oldest and youngest, yet they were so close to one another that it touched my heart. I had been aware of how precious my children were, yet I had never expressed that to them in the way that I wanted to do now. It was fun to sit on the porch of the market and watch for their return.

After the boys enjoyed some donuts and hot chocolate, we had a snow ball fight until the call finally came. It was DHQ informing me that patrol officers were at the door of Krissy's apartment and there was no answer. They had the landlord with them and wanted an okay to enter the apartment. The door was locked and there was no evidence of forced entry anywhere. I instructed them to enter, but to keep their hands in their pockets while doing a walk through and to limit the entrance of the landlord to just inside the door. In the event this was a crime scene, we had to take precautions not to contaminate it.

I held on the phone while DHQ radioed the directions to the patrol unit and within a few minutes, I was relieved to hear that Krissy was not inside. I relayed a request to the landlord to have Krissy call DHQ immediately upon her return home. She was to place an urgent request to speak to me. I then advised the good folks at the market that I was expecting another hot phone call and that it was all right to notify me whenever it came. I was hoping it wouldn't disrupt the family weekend, yet I was worried that Krissy might still be in danger, so I wanted to be able to speak with her. My wife was edgy now, anticipating the worse scenario for her, and that would be me leaving early to return to work. I told her that might not happen this time, but it was only a matter of hours until her fears were confirmed.

We were enjoying a delicious dinner of leftovers when an employee from the market came by to let me know calls had come for me. I excused myself and returned to the market with the employee. I was expecting the first message from DHQ that Krissy had called for me. The other two caught me by surprise, an emergency call from Luis and an urgent call from my captain. I didn't know how to prioritize the calls, so I chose the easy one first and called Krissy. She was fine and had been out with friends. She had not received any threats. I didn't want to frighten her, but the landlord had told her about the police entering her apartment. I told her the uniform officers were there at my request to make sure she was safe since I was out of town for the weekend. She said Luis had been calling her, saying he had to reach me immediately. I decided to make that call next.

When Luis answered the phone I could tell he was frightened. I knew he hated being in the position of helping me, while at the same time facing the reality that his life was on the line should he get caught. This time his fear showed in his voice. He said he had been at Jaden's that evening and watched Jaden pay a man to kill me. Luis had never seen the contractor before. Luis talked to Jaden about it afterward, asking him if this didn't put his entire operation at risk. Jaden told him that he had already gone to his sources in Tijuana, the Corrales cartel, because they had stopped sending couriers to Los Angeles. He fingered me as the source of their problems, and he promised them that he would take care of it. "He offered to pay them to kill you, but they refused," Luis reported.

As we talked a bit more and Luis calmed down, I was able to get the rest of the story. "Jaden said after he couldn't get help from the Corrales', he turned to his contacts in Detroit. They turned him down also. I don't know the guy who Jaden paid; I have never seen him before. He spoke with a heavy accent, probably Italian although it could have been South American. He was driving a red sports car, but he probably rented that. I got the impression he had flown in just to take the contract from Jaden. Jaden counted out $12,500 and told him another $12,500 would be paid after you were dead. He told the guy he would pay an extra $12,500 if he killed you within the week and if your body was found with a needle in your arm. He laughed and said he wanted you to go out on such a high that you wouldn't even know you were dying."

Luis wasn't any help in tracking down the hit man. His description of the guy was pretty general. I imagined he was probably terrified watching all of this while knowing he was going to report it to me. His description was of a nice looking, olive skinned, dark haired man about 5'10" with a slim build. His closing words before I hung up the phone were, "Duke, I don't know where you are, but if I was you I wouldn't go home tonight."

That was quite a phone call. I hung up and asked for a cup of coffee to gather my thoughts. I took a moment to sort out with the Lord how to handle this. I wasn't aware of feeling any fear, only a strange mix of anger and adventure. Then I called my captain at his home.

"Sorry to bother you at home on the weekend," I told him.

"Where are you now?" he asked.

When I told him, he asked me how soon I could leave. I asked if he had a crime scene for me, and he said, "I want you to get to my house as fast as you can. I'll be waiting for you." I hung up having no idea what this was about, but knowing I would have plenty of time to think on the long drive back to L.A.

• • • • •

Walking back to the cabin I only had a few minutes to decide what I was going to tell everyone. I kept remembering the parting words from Luis. I made my decision. Before entering the cabin, I paused outside to ask the Lord for his protection for my family.

Everyone was gathered inside waiting to hear from me. I had not given them specifics about my case or the phone call that threatened Krissy, but they knew something serious was going on. I asked for a moment with my wife and we went into our designated bedroom. Because she is prone to letting fear overwhelm her, I diminished the danger aspect by telling her I had to leave for L.A. to do some work for the captain. Because he and the lieutenant were personal friends, and we had socialized with them, my wife found some security in that. She knew they wouldn't call me away unless it was important.
I told her there was a guy we were all watching who was crazy and I didn't want to take any chance that the guy could find out where I lived. She wept, but she didn't lose it. I asked if she would stay the night and ride home with our friends. Then I told her that I was going to ask our friends to let her and the kids stay with them until I found out more about this crazy guy. She agreed.

When the group was together, I told them the same story. It bothered me that I might be putting our friends at risk in the event Jaden's assassin identified any of them, so I told the couple I had settled on to keep my family, Larry and Shirley, that we could have no communication until the risk was eliminated. I knew where they lived, and told them I would check in daily to provide anything needed and to let everyone know what was happening.

The whole group asked if they could leave with me, as if they could help. But the storm had grown worse and it was snowing harder. I insisted that they wait until morning so they could take their time on the drive back.

As if she had forgotten, my wife asked how long she would have at the house to pack things for her and the kids. I emphasized again that she could not slip up and even drive past the house. I would pack everything and bring it to her when she got to Larry and Shirley's.

My drive back to Los Angeles was mostly lost in dialogue with the Lord. I was processing my options, telling him I wanted to learn more about dependently trusting Him to give me what I wanted, rather than my pattern of trying to use my own resources. I was so lost in thought that the drive seemed to go quickly. The captain lived on the far west edge of the city, which meant driving all the way through the San Fernando Valley. I had been to his house on a number of occasions, mostly times of pleasure when he hosted poker parties. I had also enjoyed getting to know his oldest son who was a very good basketball player. The captain and his wife had adopted two youngsters shortly before they found out that she had breast cancer. She died after the adoption, leaving the captain with the responsibility of raising the kids. It caused him to change. He withdrew and seemed bitter over the loss of his wife. He blamed God and was guarded around me. I think he didn't know how to address his beliefs with me once he had seen how seriously I was taking my relationship with the Lord. So we never talked about personal things from that time on. I never doubted his friendship and knew that he would not betray me.

When I arrived at his home, I was surprised to see the lieutenant's car outside. I tried to think of anything I might have done to upset them and wondered if somehow they had found out about the ambush at Jaden's house. When I entered, I found both of them drinking coffee. The captain went straight to the point, "I received a call earlier tonight from the FBI. One of their reliable informants said a contract had gone out on a LAPD Robbery Homicide detective named Duke." The captain then asked me if I had any information to report to him. I told him about the calls I received in the mountains. I held my breath wondering if I would be ordered to step down from this investigation in order to keep me safe. These men were my friends and I knew they were concerned for me.

I had never known a policeman who had been through this, so I didn't know what to expect. After a brief pause, during which the two of them exchanged glances, the captain said, "Tell me what I can do for you."

Wow, what warriors these men were and they would never know how much I admired and appreciated them. I didn't have to think about what I wanted. "I want Sammy and a better undercover car." I explained that I thought Sammy wanted to partner up with me, but he's such a loyal guy that once he committed to working the robbery table he didn't want to be thought of as not keeping his word. "If you made it look as if he was ordered against his will to help me, it would make it easier all around."

The captain said he would clear that up by Monday. He also said he would have a new undercover car for me. Finally, he told me that he had already contacted Metro Division and they would have a minimum of two officers assigned to guard my house around the clock. He said they were already waiting for me at home and I should go straight there.

I asked if he had any further information on the FBI's informant. He said they were secretive about the informant, but told him the informant was reliable and had worked with the DEA on some big cases. I tried calling Dave at his house, but there was no answer. Suddenly, I was very tired.

Arriving home was surreal. It is really dark at my place since there are no street lights. It seemed especially black this night. No cars were parked outside and as I walked up the sidewalk, I could make out the shadowy figures of two men standing near the front porch.

XII. *SAMMY*

A friend loves at all times, and a brother is born for adversity.
(Proverbs 17:17)

I awoke refreshed Sunday morning. I slept well in the safety of the two Metro officers standing watch and the knowledge that my family was safe in the mountains. Each Metro officer was armed and dangerous. They carried shotguns loaded with four rounds of double- ought shells which make big holes, and a lot of them. They were assigned to 12 hour shifts, rotating with two other officers from Metropolitan Division.

I left for church, knowing that my family and friends would not be back yet. After church, I brought home a dozen donuts to enjoy with my new friends from Metro. We had our own little feast and I got to know the guys a bit better. People can say what they want about donuts, but I've never met a constipated policeman.

I went over my case with them, showing pictures of the people involved. I had nothing on the hired gun, still uncertain of his identity. The most I knew about him was his accent and the red sports car he was driving.

Early afternoon brought a call from my lieutenant. He asked, he always asked - never ordered - if I could be at the RHD offices early Monday. He said it would be important for him to know what my plan was going to be and by then he would know if the robbery team would relinquish Sammy without making a big stink.

That afternoon I kept checking at the home of Larry and Shirley until my family arrived. We were all relieved to see one another. I had dinner with them and returned home. I liked being there when the Metro officers changed shifts at 0800 and 2000 hours. I wanted the officers to know how much I appreciated them and to make sure they were well stocked with snacks and drinks. I even made them believe that my wife didn't care if they smoked inside the house. Although the temperature was dropping, we kept most of the windows open all night. Being alert meant hearing as well as seeing.

When I arrived at RHD Monday morning, I could see that I was not a popular guy with the robbery team. Sammy's partner and the robbery lieutenant just glared at me, so I figured the captain must have won this battle. Sammy's partner cornered me to say that I screwed him and that he would do his best to get Sammy back when this assignment was over.

My bosses were upbeat. They called me into the captain's office and pulled Sammy in also. We were told that we were now officially partners. We were told that our new car was available in the garage and were set free to go to work. The captain emphasized that he and the lieutenant had decided not to tell the other detectives at RHD about the contract. They felt the fewer people who knew, the safer it would be for us.

Sammy invited me to breakfast at a place where I had never been, Barragan's in Echo Park, situated on Sunset between Parker Center and the police academy. It was the beginning of a tradition for us. Whenever we were near central LA, we would stop at Barragan's for Sammy's carnitas and my huevos rancheros.

Before leaving Parker Center, we checked out our car, a new Plymouth Volare 2 door hardtop, blue, with a V-8 engine. We transferred our homicide kit into the trunk, enjoying the realization that our assignment would allow us to work from our car most of the time. I told Sammy about the freedom that our assignment gave us.

Sammy was a great listener and strategist. He wanted all of the details I could give him about the case, condensed into breakfast conversation. It was clear that our philosophy of police work was identical. We respected everyone until we identified the bad guys, and then we would bring them down at all costs. It was difficult for us to assess the urgency of the contract on my life. Other than hiding my family and keeping my house under guard, there wasn't much more we could do with that. So we laid out the things we

106

could start working on, agreeing we would put in all of the hours we could. We decided to start by hooking up with Dave. Sammy had a question that had been on my mind, "Could Luis also be an informant for the feds?" I had Luis's rap sheet and there were no arrests for federal violations, something we would have expected to see if he was helping them.

After our conversation it was clear to me that we would have a partnership based on loyalty. Neither of us would tolerate betrayal and that carried over to our personal lives. I was confident that Sammy would not be influenced by the temptations of the women in this case which caused so many problems for me working alone.

● ● ● ● ●

Dave was eager to meet with us. We drove to his office, one that Sammy was familiar with because of his experience in working narcotics cases. When we sat down, Dave apologized for being out of contact for the holiday weekend. He had been in Reno. He didn't receive the message I had left on his home phone until late last night when he returned. He didn't know the identity of the FBI informant but was told it was not Luis. He said some of his agents had tried to contact him because they knew he was working to develop a case on Jaden and figured he might know the target of the contract. "When they couldn't reach me they called RHD and were put in touch with your boss."

Dave told us his primary contacts in our case were Barry, arrested with Max and now housed at Terminal Island, and Malibu George who had set up the buy-bust operation. Dave said he would arrange meetings for us right away and would sit in with us if we so desired.

I called Bob at INS from Dave's office and filled him in on everything that was happening. He said he was going to find out if there was any way for him to get Hannah back into custody. These contacts were a tremendous help. They took the case personally, just the way Sammy did.

Sammy and I then set out for West Hollywood so he could see where Jaden lived. The house still appeared as if no one was there. We pulled out our Thomas Guide and followed the most direct path we could from West Hollywood to where Max's body had been buried. Sammy asked me to show him how I climbed down the hill using the vines. Funny.

We then looked for a place to use for an office in the valley so we could spread out our paperwork and do some reading, note keeping and planning. Sammy lived on the east side of the San Fernando Valley, while I lived on the west. In the middle, near the city of San Fernando, we found a small fire station. We dropped in and spoke with the captain, telling him that we were looking for a place to work from, and he invited us to use his fire station. He walked us into the kitchen and introduced us to his men. All firemen start with the same question, "Do you guys know what policemen and firemen have in common?" We already knew the punch line: that they both want to be firemen, so before they could spring it, I said, "Since policemen are heterosexual, it must be something else," and from the laughter I knew we were accepted to work on their turf. They gave us a schedule of meal times and invited us to eat with them anytime. The only thing they wanted from us was to tell them about the case we were working.

We left to go to Sammy's home. He had ridden to work with his robbery partner. On the way, Sammy directed me to a salvage yard where old cars were dismantled. Our new car had regular license plates, but they were still registered to the city. We walked through the yard and removed two sets of license plates from cars destined for destruction. Outside the yard, we put one of the sets on our undercover vehicle and put the other set into our homicide kit in the trunk. Now, no matter who might take our license number, it could never be traced to us. We had cold plates.

I drove Sammy home and met his family. Like me, he had four kids that were happy to see him. We had a lot to do in a very short time, so I told Sammy I'd pick him up early the next morning. Driving home, I had a hard time expressing my thanksgiving for being provided such a great partner. I reflected on how similarly we approached our work, and then as if to keep me humble, I thought I could hear the Lord whisper that Sammy was better looking and smarter. I smiled, but the truth was that he could be a double for Clark Gable.

On the way home, I picked up a phone recording machine. I wanted the Metro officers to be able to screen all incoming calls. I also stopped to see my family. My wife had kept the kids out of school until she talked to me to see if it was safe to send them. I told her it was. I was wrong.

XIII. *DESPERADO*

Contend, O Lord, with those who contend with me. Fight against those who fight against me. (Psalm 35:1)

First thing next morning, Sammy and I went to a post office in the valley. We convinced the postmaster to let me open a post office box without filling out the paperwork that is normally required. This eliminated the chance of a postal employee getting my personal information. Then I had all mail to my house changed to the street address for the post office.

We began what we knew would be a long day of interviews, starting with a drive to the Terminal Island federal prison in the San Pedro area of Los Angeles. We met Dave there. He had arranged to have Barry pulled out to a private interview room, reducing the chance that other inmates would identify Barry as a snitch. We all knew that doesn't reduce the threat by much, as inmates work as trustees in almost every part of the prison and they are conduits for the latest news and rumors.

Like informants are inclined to do, Barry started off to see if we would go for his bullshit, "I won't trust the feds, but I can make LAPD's case for you if you guarantee that I'll be deported to Canada instead of taking the fall for this DEA beef. I'm in danger here. Dave lied to Carl and Max and told them that I'm a snitch. If you can get me away from DEA, I'll tell you who killed Max."

I knew Sammy had worked many cases using informants and he knew the same about me. We told Barry that we wouldn't promise him anything in return for helping us. Only after we evaluated what he had to say would we make a decision on whether to help him. Sammy added, "In other words, you have to trust us and we will know if you lie. If you do, we will hurt you."

Barry could tell right away that he couldn't bluff us. We figured he might give us a little bit just to keep us from walking away. "You guys are on the right track. Jaden killed Max for screwing up his business. Max had moved in on Jaden's connections and

110

was taking things away from him. Max had some strong backing in Chicago and there wasn't much that Jaden could do. Jaden sent Max to point A to pick up some cash and then to point B to deliver some H. He had been working for Jaden, but Jaden didn't realize how well-liked Max had become. People liked doing business with him. He also had some connections with a lot of older movie stars. He told me about a number of big parties he was attending in Beverly Hills. Max said Hannah had introduced him to the senator who enjoyed being invited to the Hollywood parties. In return, the senator offered help in making it easier for Max to bring stuff in from Mexico." Barry then turned to me and said, "There are some heavyweights you have to watch out for. I'll tell you more if we can make a deal."

We told Barry we would think about it. Outside, Dave agreed with us that Barry didn't have anything that would help us. Dave took us from Terminal Island to Malibu where he introduced us to George, who lived in a nice place on the beach. Dave told us that George was a very intelligent guy who had a background in finances. He had made a lot of money in business, but like many smart guys, drugs were his undoing. The house belonged to one of the friends George had a business relationship with from his days in the banking world.

After introductions, George jumped right in. "I've heard about the contract and called a friend in the vending machine business. Dominick and his partners were becoming successful, but they made the mistake of borrowing start-up money from a source they didn't realize had organized crime connections. When Dom was visited by some guys who said they were his new partners, he resisted. His original partners were soon found dead, so he reconsidered and signed his business over to his new partners. He's got some good OC connections now. I told him I had heard about Jaden looking for someone to make a hit on a cop and that I knew someone who would take the contract. Dom told me to stay out of it because Jaden had already given the hit to someone. I asked if he knew who it was. He said it was a contractor from out of the country. He said whenever the guy is in town, he likes to hang out at The Ball in Santa Monica. He said he didn't know the guys name, but after taking the contract he heard a guy had been recruited from the bay area to come to LA to help with the job. Jaden paid $12,500 up front with another $12,500 to be paid when it's done. There's a bonus if it's done within a week. Dom said Jaden put himself in a cross with his connections by trying to get Detroit to take the contract. When they refused, he turned to his connections in Tijuana. Now everybody thinks Jaden is too out of control to work with. They believe you've driven him crazy and he can't be trusted. The more his dope dries up, the crazier he gets. Dom told me to stay far away from Jaden because when the hit goes down the police will put heat on anyone they think knows Jaden."

We asked George if he felt comfortable staying in touch with Dominick to feed us any new information he can get. He said he would try. We bought lunch for Dave at Paradise Cove in Malibu, and then Sammy and I left to visit Krissy.

The drive south along Pacific Coast Highway was beautiful. It was a sunny, crisp day and we could see the waves breaking and the many surfers riding them. As we passed a pickup truck with gardening tools in the back, Sammy wondered aloud what it would be like to cut lawns for a living. "No complications," he mused, "you just do a job and at the end of the day it's finished and you go home. Nothing like what we do."

As we cut across Topanga Canyon toward the valley, we received a call from RHD. Luis was waiting to meet with us at Two Guys Pizza in Hollywood. Krissy would have to wait. We had already used up most of the daylight for this day. Sammy stopped the car at a hippy restaurant in the canyon and we used the pay phone to call the pizza parlor. Luis was there and said he would wait for us to make the drive. It was dark when we arrived.

$$\bullet \ \bullet \ \bullet \ \bullet \ \bullet$$

Luis appeared threatened by Sammy, almost as if he could sense that Sammy had much more experience in narcotics than I did. I was surprised that he had picked a small pizza joint in the middle of Hollywood for a meet. Even though Sammy and I almost always wore levis, anyone who wasn't blind would make us for the police. And Jaden knew who I was, so I figured Luis must feel pretty safe about being seen in public with us. He started by telling us that Jaden had left town and was going to stay away until after I was killed. He figured that would remove him as a suspect in my death.

Luis kept an eye on Sammy as he spoke, "Jaden's Mexican connections refuse to come to LA. He had to go to San Diego himself to pick up a shipment. He's on his way to Oregon and from there he'll fly it into Detroit. He's going to stay there until he hears that you have been killed. He says he's in the mafia, working for a guy named Tony. We had to laugh at that, "Luis, everybody in the mafia is named Tony."

Luis boastfully continued by saying this Tony owns race tracks. "Jaden says he's the mafia godfather on the west coast. That's all I've heard about the contract."

Luis asked if we had talked to Timmy yet. "He was living with Jaden when Max was killed and might know something." Sammy decided to test Luis by telling him that we had talked to Timmy and he told us that Luis knew who killed Jaden. Luis became defensive and said, "I'm doing my best to help. I'm taking a lot of chances for you guys." He then diverted away by telling us about a girlfriend in the Marina. "She got in a beef with Jaden and he beat her so bad that she has been hospitalized in really bad shape. She won't talk to the police because she's afraid Jaden will have her killed. The beef was over some money she owed Jaden for dope. He's gone over the edge."

It was getting so late now that I knew I wasn't going to have time to see my family. I drove Sammy home so I could keep the car. We would keep digging tomorrow. I used his home phone to call my wife. She had sent the kids to school this day and said they seemed to be fine except for my daughter. My wife said, "I told her about the crazy guy because I want her to be careful. I warned her not to tell anybody." I asked how she took it and my wife said she showed no reaction and still seems distant.

When I left Sammy's I was so tired that I wasn't sleepy. I drove back to West Hollywood and parked on the strip near the Rainbow. I just watched people as they walked along the sidewalk. I got out of the car and sat on the fender where I could get a closer look. I had tried so hard to imagine what the killer was thinking in my murder cases, that it sometimes took over my thoughts. Even though I hated it, I couldn't shut it out right away. As I watched the pedestrians, my mind started imagining what each was thinking and how vulnerable they were to some savage taking advantage of them. I could actually picture them being dissected in the morgue. This always made me feel creepy and I thought it must be like the guys I knew who were addicted to watching pornography. Once the pictures get in your head, it is not easy to get them out. I told myself, "Duke, you're addicted to crime scene porn."

I got back in the car and confessed to the Lord that I was slipping back into my old life purpose of being consumed by my work. I started driving home, looking forward to spending some time in the scriptures. Then, as if a reminder from the Lord, a country station played a release that I had not heard before. I wept as the closing lyrics were sung, "Desperado, why don't you come to your senses? Come down from your fences; open the gate. It may be raining, but there's a rainbow above you; you'd better let somebody love you before it's too late." Tears were blurring my vision, making it hard to drive. I remembered taking my daughter in my arms on the day she came home from the hospital. At that moment I had experienced an epiphany of sorts, being vividly aware that she would grow up to be a woman who had been shaped by the way I fathered her. Wow, had I dropped the ball big time after those early years when I doted over her. She was my first-born and the apple of my eye in those early years. I showed her off to everyone. She was daddy's girl and she knew it. Now, she feels that she's not valuable anymore.

• • • • •

When I arrived home, I laid across my bed fully dressed, feeling lonely and wondering what my daughter believed about me now. I was asleep before I could shut my mind off and had a dream of taking my daughter to visit my dad when she was four. My dad had really softened when he was with her. It was like she got close to her grandpa in a way that I never got to experience with my dad.

I had no way of knowing how much I was going to need my rest for the events of the next day.

XIV. *KIDNAP*

The horse is prepared for the day of battle, but victory belongs to the Lord. (Proverbs 21:31)

I was on the phone to my wife early the next morning. My daughter had already left for school. My wife pleaded with me to get home in time to see her and the kids. I told her I would try, but I hung up in a rush. I was out the door to pick up Sammy. We had decided to look for Timmy this day.

I had gotten so busy that I hadn't talked to Rose for over a week. On my way to Sammy's I received a radio call that Rose had left a message on my home phone to call her. The Metro guys had forwarded the message to me via RHD. When I arrived at Sammy's, I made the call.

I would never concern Rose about the contract or my family hiding in a safe house. She had enough on her plate and already worried about us too much. She sounded excited this morning for good reason. She had spoken to some musician friends of Max. They told her that a month before his death, he had showed up at their home near San Bernardino. He had spent some time with them and they asked him to join their band. He was worried about a Canadian gig he already signed a contract for, so he put off taking their offer. However, he attended one of their concerts, and said he had chosen to give his life to Christ. Rose fell apart as she told me. "That was the last time they saw him. He asked them if they wanted to do the Canadian job with him. They declined. They said he was conflicted by this because he didn't know if he could get out of the Canadian job. He was very remorseful over some of the things he was doing with his life. At least this gives me the hope that I will see my boy again someday," she said. She asked me to fill her in on the investigation and each one in my family. Since we had much to do this day, I kept it as brief as I could, not an easy task with Rose.

I had collected phone information on every person involved in the case, including all of their phone bills. It required a separate file and we worked on it at the fire station trying to see if we could find any leads. We called Krissy to see if she could direct us to Timmy. She had seen him the day before and he invited her to one of his swing parties in the Hollywood hills. She had saved the address and gave it to us. I asked her what happens at a swing party. She laughed.

"It's just a sex orgy, married couples swap partners, single people ball one another, and gay guys and lesbians show up also."

"Will my partner be safe there?" I asked, loud enough for Sammy and the firemen to hear.

Before we could leave, we received a call from Dave. George's court date was the day before. He had already pled out on his case. Because of his cooperation with DEA, he was sentenced to two years, the minimum penalty for his crime. Dave was arranging for him to do his time at the new federal facility in Pleasanton. He said George wanted to talk to us some more. We told him we would work a trip into our schedule and call him back. We had brunch with the firemen. They liked challenging us to play in their cribbage tournaments, but we didn't have time this day.

• • • • •

It was getting close to noon by the time we found the address for Timmy's party. It was a nice corner residence with a landscaped yard, not what we were expecting. By the number of cars on the street it looked as if there was a lot of swinging going on. Except for Timmy's old clunker of a car, one that Krissy had described for us, the other cars were nice.

We walked up the sidewalk and tried the front door. It was unlocked, so we walked in. I had pulled Timmy's rap sheet and we had a mug shot of him. Everything we knew about him led us to believe he was a sleazy pervert and a con artist, always looking for a fast and easy way to take money from his marks.

Inside the house, it took a minute for our eyes to adjust as the windows had been covered and the rooms had been separated by drapes. There were all sorts of crude sounds coming from behind the drapes. Before we could walk in on the action, Timmy stepped from a side room with another man and asked who we were. The man said he owned the house and unless we were invited, he would have to put us out. I told him we weren't leaving and suggested that he call the police, "We could probably get the vice squad here if you'd like." The man shrunk back into the room he came from.

We took Timmy into the kitchen where we were alone. He didn't disappoint our prejudgment of him. As soon as he opened his mouth he convinced us that everything we had heard about him was true. He started by presenting himself as a legitimate entrepreneur and bragged about his concept of private swing clubs as if he thought we were going to invest in a venture he believed would sweep the country. We told him we'd have a look around before we left, but it was only to watch him sweat.

Timmy had a story, but it didn't tell us anything. He said he was living with Jaden and Hannah when Max was killed. "I didn't like Max, so I stayed away from him. He was a disgusting human being, always sponging off other people," Timmy said, as if he was describing himself. "I had met Hannah at one of my swing parties. She's drop dead gorgeous and was a big hit. She introduced me to Jaden. I knew he took care of her, but I never knew what he did for a living. It looked to me like he and Max were in some sort of business together. Hannah told me that Max's body had been found buried on Mulholland Drive. "I asked Jaden if he knew what had happened to Max. He gave me a cold look and walked away without saying anything. His look told me not to ask him again."

Timmy slipped in the name of his attorney as if to impress us. I not only knew his lawyer, I had played poker with him. I told Sammy we could find out all we wanted to know about Timmy from his attorney, and we left after telling Timmy we would see him again, maybe at another one of his parties. He was standing outside looking paranoid as we drove off. Sammy and I thought about using a hose to spray ourselves off.

● ● ● ● ●

Before we got out of the hills, we received a radio call to phone the office immediately. We weren't far from the Hollywood police station so we drove there and used the phone in the offices of Hollywood Juvenile, across the street from the police station.

Sammy made the call and handed the phone to me. The lieutenant told me to call my wife at the safe house right away. He said something had happened and I would need to get home right away.

My wife was waiting for my call and she was angry. It was past time for my daughter to be home from school. She asked me why I hadn't told her that my brother was coming from his home in Santa Monica to pick her up. I didn't know what she was talking about, and told her I was really busy. I asked her to start at the beginning so I would know what was happening. She had received a call from one of the office personnel at my daughter's junior high school, just before the school day ended. The woman said a man identifying himself as my brother had come to the school, and asked to pick up my daughter. The woman refused, and the man left before she could ask him any questions. The woman said that she called my daughter to the office to ask her what was going on, and that she appeared frightened and asked to leave school early. She was given permission, but my wife said she hadn't come home.

I told my wife to call the school, and ask the office personnel to remain until I could get there. Then Sammy and I left for the valley. Our little undercover car could really fly, and we made good time getting to the school. Lois, the woman who called my wife was waiting. She told us that during the last hour of school there was a student working the office desk. A tall, well dressed man entered the office and asked for my daughter by name. He said he was my brother, and that I had asked him to pick her up and take her home. The girl told him she would call my daughter to come to the office. The man said he had left his car running, and would be waiting for her outside.

Lois said she was walking through the office, and overheard part of the conversation. Since she knew I was a policeman, she intervened and stopped my daughter from being summoned. She went outside to ask the man for some identification, but he drove away when he saw her walking toward the car. She was unable to get a license number, and was very remorseful for her failure. I was so grateful that I gave her a hug. She said there were two men, and they were in a red sports car.

I had not anticipated an attempt on one of my kids. It infuriated me. Sammy brought me to my senses by asking me where we could start looking for my daughter. I had been so absent from my family that I didn't even know who her friends were. I asked Lois, and then called my wife to see if she could help with some names. We checked a couple of addresses where some girls lived, but no one claimed to have any knowledge of her whereabouts.

Since it was now early evening, I told Sammy I would take him home, and then keep trying to contact students by phone. Sammy wanted to stay and help me look, but I felt like I was just going to be wasting my time. On the drive to his house, we talked about our frustration over Jaden's sudden disappearance. Almost simultaneously, it came to our minds that we could take care of things by hunting Jaden down and killing him ourselves.
What a delicious thought for me. We would know how to conceal the body in a location that, if it should ever be discovered, would end up being a case assigned to us. When we arrived at Sammy's, I called my wife. She still hadn't heard from Alice. I called Krissy, Luis and Dave to ask for help in finding Jaden. I then sped across the valley toward home. It was almost dark as I drove down the narrow road near my house. I could see a small group of kids crossing the road ahead. As I neared, I saw that one of the kids was my daughter. I pulled to the shoulder and jumped out of the car, calling her by the pet name I had given her as an infant. She looked at me and hesitated. Her friends took off running, shouting for her to follow.

I started toward her. I held my arms out, saw her pause, and then she made a dash into the wash. I chased her for a brief way, but had to stop. My heart was breaking, and I couldn't run anymore. It was horrible to see my daughter running away from me. I just stood and watched her until she was out of sight. She didn't look back.

I was less than a block from my house, so I went there to tell the Metro officers what had happened. Now their job would be more risky since any signs of an intruder would have to be carefully checked out before they could take action. This put them in the position of hesitating before acting, not a good thing for their safety. I was glad my wife had told my daughter that I had guards at home. I hoped that it would keep her from carelessly approaching the house. Then I remembered she was a teenager.

I called Sammy from home to brief him. He told me he had an idea that he wanted to talk over with me the next morning. I knew that Sammy and I agreed on the need to frighten suspects into making mistakes, but I also knew that neither of us would hurt anyone in the process. That night I went back to the bible to consider what God meant by saying that vengeance belonged to him. Scripture makes it perfectly clear that when God makes justice his purpose, he delivers a payback to his enemies that Sammy and I couldn't come close to accomplishing. Scripture states that he has empowered authorities like the police and military to exact vengeance for him against the wicked. The dilemma seemed to be between the good desire for payback and the temptation to exact it ourselves. I was at peace knowing that the most I could do in this life would be to kill the wicked, but that God deals with the evil after this life is over, and his judgment goes on forever. He knows how to exact vengeance perfectly, he even mentions letting the wicked swim in their own excrement. I slept after telling him I was sorry for thinking that I could do anything better than he.

XV. _BILLY_

Better is a poor man who walks in his integrity, than he who is perverse in speech and is a fool. (Proverbs 19:1)

The next morning kept the pace at a hectic level. It was Saturday, and I was anxious to pick up Sammy and find out what he had been thinking the night before. However, as soon as I left the house I received a radio call to return home. When I got back, the Metro officers said a call had come in from a girl who might know something about my daughter. As it turned out, she lived just a couple of blocks north of us.

When I got to her house, I was greeted by her adult brother with whom she lived. I had never seen this girl before. She identified herself as Kelley, a classmate of my daughter. She was also 14 years old. She and my daughter shared a locker at school. My daughter had told her about my dangerous situation. I noticed that she resembled my daughter in her physical build: tall, slender and pretty. "Yesterday when I left school on the bus, I saw some creepy guys in a red car watching me. When I got home, my brother and his wife left for the store. A couple of minutes later, this guy came to the door. It looked like the guy I saw in the red car. He acted friendly and asked if I knew where your daughter was. I told him she was probably home, duh! I must have sounded pretty sarcastic. He asked me if I knew where you lived. When I said no he started to leave, and then said he was your brother. He said he hadn't been to your house for a while and was having trouble finding it. I closed and locked the door so I didn't see how he left. I didn't think too much about it until I remembered what your daughter had told me about you. I had your home number and my brother told me I should call you."

Kelley described the suspect as white and tall, just a little shorter than me and not as stocky. He had dark hair with gray around the edges and was wearing a gray suit and tie and sunglasses. He had no accent. I figured the Italian must be driving the red car, but lying back since his English was not good. That's probably why he recruited help from the bay area. Kelley said she had no idea why my daughter ran away or where she might be, but she would check with friends and call me if she found anything out.

• • • • •

I called Sammy to tell him I was on the way. He had received a call from Bob at INS with more news. There was so much to catch up on that to save time, Sammy was going to drive to the fire station.

The firemen had found out from Sammy what we were dealing with, and were very sympathetic to me when I arrived. They had finished breakfast, but insisted on cooking for Sammy and me. Bob had informed Sammy that Hannah's deportation hearing had been moved up to Monday. He was such a great guy that he had found a way to place her back in custody and had picked her up at Jaden's place. He said she was alone in the house when he arrested her. He booked her at the West Hollywood Sheriff's station. He had left instructions that cleared us to visit her.

Sammy and I were both stumped at how a junkie like Jaden could be connected, and we agreed it was more likely that he had no connection with the mob, but kept the illusion alive to give him some juice on the street. Sammy felt that even if it were true that he had connections, it would be very unlikely that there would be an organized crime hit against me. He said it was his experience that these gangsters normally do not mess with police officers and their families.

I was surprised when Sammy told me that he had a close friend who was connected with the mob. His wife's cousin, Billy, a Sicilian, grew up in a tough Italian neighborhood in Brooklyn. As a kid he did odd jobs for the gangsters who controlled his neighborhood. He ran numbers and stole anything that wasn't nailed down. He ended up as a mob soldier. After Billy's release from Terminal Island on a federal hi-jacking charge, Billy decided to stay in Los Angeles. Sammy said their friendship developed during family gatherings. Out of respect for Sammy and his position as a police officer, Billy would not socialize with him outside of family affairs. Sammy told me that Billy was the most honest person he knew in his family. He thought it would be smart of us to get an expert's opinion on our case and said he would work on arranging a meeting with Billy. He made a call while I finished eating, and said Billy agreed to meet us after dark at a bar near LAX.

• • • • •

I was torn between interviewing Hannah and going home to look for my daughter. But since I had no idea where my daughter might be, Sammy and I headed for West Hollywood.

When Hannah saw me I couldn't tell if she was afraid or angry. Maybe it was a little of both. It was great having a partner with me that I could trust completely. I knew I had much better leverage with his presence. By their demeanor, it was apparent that the people we talked to somehow sensed he was able to see through their lies as he sat quietly listening to them.

We started by asking Hannah what country she would be living in next. "I'm going to Switzerland. My dad is an ambassador from there and he will give me anything I want. Jaden is already on his way there to meet me. I stay with him because I love him. We are both heroin addicts, but I can quit whenever I want.

"I'm going to get clean and write a book about dope and prostitution and crooked cops in Los Angeles. When I'm not using, I can type over 100 words a minute." Glaring directly at me she concluded with, "I want to be drug free to be sure I spell your name right."

That led me to ask if she was a member of the horny lawyers club. She laughed. "You're talking about Peter and Harry. They prey on the working girls so they don't have to go without sex. They could never get a girl on their own; although I'm sure they are switch-hitters, so they always have their boy-toys.

"But I'm not a working girl, at least not like Krissy. That's why I couldn't live with her. She is a factory worker, an assembly line for sex. She makes good money, but she works hard to earn it. My book is going to be about how I learned to play the politicians. That's where the real money is, and you only have to bed down one guy at a time. I can name names. I've bedded down guys from the DA's office all the way up to the state level. The biggest guy I've balled is the senator. He uses the 9000 Sunset building because it's owned by some bad boys from Las Vegas. I'll say this for the senator, of all the politicians I've balled, he was the only one who would snort coke with me. Drugs scared the others. The senator kept me for a long time, but got scared when my habit got too big. He's going to be the president some day."

It was obvious that Hannah enjoyed talking about her own significance, so we turned it to asking how she ended up with a creep like Jaden. "Jaden is easy and he'll do anything for me. We got married in Vegas. He had connections to all of the dope we wanted until you came along and screwed things up. I told him it would be better to be nice to you than to make you an enemy. He's not smart enough to see that. You knew you had him. Yeah, he killed Max, but you can't do anything about it. I'll never testify against him and we'll never come back to L.A. After we married, we took out big life insurance policies on each other. I'll be a rich woman if anything happens to Jaden. I never liked Max. I could see he wanted to move ahead of Jaden. I tried to tell Jaden but he liked treating Max like his flunky. Then when Max started taking his connections, it was too late for Jaden to do anything but kill him. After Max was busted with Carl and Barry there were rumors about one of them being a snitch. Jaden made Max believe that he trusted him. He told Max he was going to find out who the snitch was and take care of him and that Max could watch. It was just a set-up. Jaden told me he whacked him in the head with an axe while they were outside. He didn't say exactly where it happened."

I asked if anyone else helped Jaden, like Luis or Timmy. "I don't know. Jaden wanted me to believe he was strong enough to do things alone, but he wasn't. He was so weak that I could kick his ass. He would push girls around, but never a guy. We called Timmy the dog. He was such a sex pervert that when we hired a maid he kept raping her. He drugged her up so much that she started acting just like us, doing drugs all day and not working. We had to let her go."

Sammy lit up a cigarette for himself and offered one to Hannah. He asked her why she wouldn't want to clean up and stay in Los Angeles. "Because I want to be with Jaden. I've always cooperated with the police. Things would be different if Jaden would have listened to me, but he hates Duke so much that he can't think straight."

"What's he going to do about Duke?"

"He's put out a contract to a guy from out of the country, I don't know who. Jaden wanted to protect me on that one. That's the reason he's hiding somewhere else and he wants me with him."

I asked her if she didn't care what happened to a nice guy like me. She locked eyes with me and said, "You're pretty cute, but you're not cut out for my world. I think you can take care of yourself. I know you guys have been around enough to have built-in lie detectors. You know I'm telling you the truth. So that's it, please leave me alone now. This INS beef is not going to be easy. My mom lives here and is married to a federal judge. This is going to be hard on her. I hope I never see you again."

We had everything we were going to get from Hannah, but I was curious about one more thing and I figured Sammy was too. "You just told us about a contract as if you knew we already were aware of it. How would we have found out?"

"I always assume you guys know everything that I know. That's why I'm not afraid to tell you the truth. You had to know, you talk to too many people."

I used the phone in the sheriff's office to call Luis. I asked him if he had heard any more about Jaden. He said, "I heard that Jaden is offering the hit man even more money to kill you before Monday. He wants to come back for Hannah's hearing and he wants you out of the way." Luis still had no information on who the hit man could be. We went back into the jail to where Hannah was being processed for her transfer to county jail. I told her to tell Jaden that I know where he is, and I'm coming to get him. We would track all of her calls from the jail to see if she tried to call him, but the only call she made was for a taxi.

Sammy and I left to get some dinner and meet Billy. We got to the bar at 8pm. It was foggy near the airport and the exterior of the bar reminded me of a scene from Casablanca. We stepped inside and Sammy looked around until he saw Billy at a table. There weren't any other patrons at tables, just a few folks at the bar. Billy sat still as we approached. The table had chairs around it and the table top had a strange shape, something that caused me to momentarily flash back to junior high geometry class and a teacher trying to convince us that someday what we were learning would be very valuable. I thought of the best student in the class, Bryant Jewell, and wondered if he had opened a manufacturing business to make table tops for bars. Sammy introduced me to Billy.

Billy was a big man with a big head and huge hands. He remained expressionless as he extended his right hand. I thought he looked familiar, but then I remembered I had recently seen The Godfather movie and he could have played any of the characters. He held up his hand and as soon as he snapped his fingers the bartender appeared. Billy ordered drinks for each of us while Sammy and I sat down.

Sammy briefed Billy on our case and my situation. Billy listened stoically. When Sammy came to the attempt on my daughter, I noticed a change. Billy asked me to go over that part again. When I did, he said he would tell us how he would take care of Jaden. At first I wasn't sure what he meant, but I wasn't going to interrupt. Billy's physical appearance made it clear that you wouldn't want to upset him.

Billy leaned back, lit up a cigarette, and after a cough he leaned forward and began talking. "Jaden is full of shit and is playing a dangerous game by throwing around the idea that he is mob connected. That by itself indicates he's probably not." Every drag that Billy took on his cigarette was followed by coughing. He continued, "But he's made a move that can't be ignored. The man you need to talk to is in the San Diego area. His name is Tony Marino. You guys can figure out how to approach him; just remember if he agrees to see you that he's very high up and deserving of respect. His family is big in many ways, including politics. The feds just sent a couple of his brothers to prison, so he'll be cautious about meeting with you. Remember, he's the boss. Whatever else you do, don't try to bullshit him. If he suspects that, you're through. Be straight with him and tell him the truth. I can guarantee that if he believes what you say is true, he will not be very happy with this piece of shit, Jaden. The rest should take care of itself. Try reaching him at his office in Del Mar. It's near the race track.

Once we broke the ice with Billy it was fun talking to him. He told some stories of life in Brooklyn where he grew up without his dad. "He abandoned me and mom to run off with his whore. He was a made-man. He never gave us a penny after he left, so I had to earn enough for me and mom to live. I had some buddies and we pulled some robberies, but eventually robbed the wrong business and the mob found us. They almost killed me but because they knew my dad, they let me live. I wanted to be made after that, so I worked for a sponsor. My job is exactly like yours. I was in charge of keeping the peace and making sure everybody did the right thing, like paying their gambling debts. I never liked to hurt anybody but you guys know that sometimes violence is the only thing that works. I worked Vegas in the years when you never had to worry about crime. Folks could leave their valuables in their rooms, and not think twice about something being taken. The few times it happened, we would find the thief and make sure he never stole again. So we do the same job, I just work for different bosses than you."

Billy was easy to like. In telling his story, he mentioned his wife and being raised in the Catholic Church in New York. When he mentioned the church, he didn't sound as if it was a good experience. I remembered what I had learned from scripture about everyone having a belief system in the heart, so I asked Billy what he believed about God. He was very animated and said, "Oh, I definitely believe God is real, and that I will see him when I die. I'm going to rip his head off and spit down his throat for how the priests treated me and mom after dad left us."

All I could do was smile, hearing Billy describe a belief about God that was not based on scripture, but from his life experience. Sammy let me know that it was late. I told Billy I hoped to have the chance to visit with him again. He seemed to like the idea and asked me to let him know if he could do anything more to help me with my daughter.

• • • • •

On the drive home, Sammy filled me in with some family stories about Billy and the first time they had met. We were worn out, and decided to take Sunday off for some rest and hit it hard on Monday, the day of Hannah's deportation hearing and maybe the return of Jaden.

I told Sammy I would start trying to contact Tony the next day and if he agreed to meet us it would be on his terms, even if it meant making the trip tomorrow. We both understood that we would do whatever was necessary. I was praying that the Lord would keep my daughter safe and bring her home to me on Sunday.

XVI. *DEPORTED*

Woe to those who call evil good, and good evil; who substitute darkness for light, and light for darkness; who substitute bitter for sweet, and sweet for bitter! (Isaiah 5:20)

I would have slept all day had the Metro officers not awakened me at their change of shift. I was really slow getting up. I had become hyper about making sure no one was following me, and I took the same precautions this morning as I picked up my family and took us to church. I let the guys know that if my daughter came home to hold her for me, and I'd be back right after lunch.

Church was not a good experience for me. I was tired and tried to excuse my irritability based on that. But the pastor went on about how magnificent God was compared to us, true of course, but he took it to an illustration of pulling out a jar of ants to show how God looked down at the insignificance of mankind. This really disturbed me because it is unbiblical. It seemed to me this pastor had only read chapter one of Genesis and never turned the page to see what the Lord did in chapter two.

My wife could see that I was disturbed, but she didn't know why it bothered me so. I hated that folks might get the impression that God was far away and indifferent. That was the tactic that Satan used with Adam and Eve, and couldn't be further from the truth.

It was pleasant to see Larry and Shirley and other friends. They were doing a lot to help us while making it appear as if it was no inconvenience at all. I included Larry and Shirley, and took my family to lunch. We went to a local breakfast place. Even though I was preoccupied worrying about my daughter, I couldn't help but pick up on the conversation when others complained about the morning message. I heard someone say it seemed that something was missing in the way the pastor taught. I wondered to myself what the pastor really believed about God and his word. As I reflected on this, I felt something stirring inside of me about helping people understand the themes that could be tracked through the whole bible.

I had experienced a similar discomfort in talking to police officers who had found out through the grapevine that I had become a Christian. Some had approached me with questions about how I could be so aggressive in my pursuit of bad guys and claim to be a Christian. It was apparent to me that the failure of studying the whole bible had caused a twisted theology for many, one that failed to see God's strong warnings to never blur the lines between right and wrong, good and evil. God doesn't compromise. He fights for the right thing and for his purpose.

Liberalism despises God's word, both in the church and in politics, so that right and wrong are interchangeable. That way, liberals don't see anything worth fighting for other than their own self-interest. Maybe that's why there are so many liberal lawyers who would be out of work if they couldn't find a loophole or nuance that muddied the intent of the law.

Officers who would ask me about their conflict between relentlessly hunting down bad guys and some strange idea of being nice, had such a skewed theology that I thought they should not be in law enforcement. A moment's hesitation in the heat of battle could be a fatal mistake for them or somebody else, and I told them so. Liberalism was making everyone afraid to fight, a strange awakening for a guy who grew up bearing the identity of a coward.

But, I still had to be careful not to come across as an arrogant fool, something I had mastered through the years to cover up my insecurities, so I tried to keep my mouth shut until I talked things through with the Lord. I always ended up with the same question: who was going to fight for him if people didn't want anything badly enough to fight. Remembering the first crime scene kept me on track.

●●●●●

After lunch I went home and tried calling Tony. I placed a call to the number Billy had provided. Of course, no one was there; it was Sunday after all. I was secretly relieved, as it gave me some

131

time to relax. I watched some football with the troops at my house. We had a beer and some snacks.

A noise in the back yard drew our attention. The troops grabbed their weapons and immediately made a maneuver to cover one another. One slipped out the front door to recon the front of the house, the other approached the patio slider leading to the rear, being careful not to expose himself. The back yard was walled on two sides with a chain link fence separating our yard from an open field.

We had trees and shrubs planted on our side of the fence. I had a pit bull that stayed in the back yard. The kids loved to ride him like a pony. One look at him would keep anyone away, although he would never harm an intruder, unless he was carrying another dog.

I saw the dog run into the shrubs, and when no one ran out I figured my daughter was home. The first officer had time to circle to the back. I shouted out to my daughter. Sure enough, she sheepishly crept out from the shrubbery. What a wonderful surprise to see her. I went outside and grabbed her. As I held her, I realized that I had shied away from showing her any affection when she reached adolescence. I was around so many perverts that I was afraid to appropriately touch my own daughter. I realized now how that set her up to confuse a safe and loving touch from her dad with an unsafe touch from someone telling her they loved her, when all they wanted was to take advantage of her. My family needed to experience what it meant for me to be safe and protective. I had a lot of work to do to make up for the past, this moment was a good start.

She told me that she had run away because she had failed to complete a homework assignment that was due last week. Afraid of the trouble she would be in, she stole another girl's project and presented it as her own. When she got caught, she left school and was walking with some friends when she saw me driving toward her. She was caught between telling me the truth and getting busted, or just running. She said she was sorry she ran, and I told her I was sorry that I hadn't loved her better. She wanted to stay with me all day, but that was impossible. I let her hang out with me and the troops for a while, and then took her to Larry and Shirley's. I was glad to see that everyone rallied around her. I felt things would be all right, so I left her there and returned to the house. I called Sammy to let him know that some of the pressure was off.

● ● ● ● ●

I picked up Sammy Monday morning. I called Tony's office when we arrived at the fire station. His secretary answered and said he wasn't there. I identified myself, and told her I had an urgent matter to discuss with him. She assured me she would deliver the message as soon as he arrived. I left the numbers for RHD and DHQ.

Next, Sammy called Bob. He was already in the hearing for Hannah. Another message left, and now we were stuck waiting for return calls. We left the fire station phone number with DHQ, so they could reach us as soon as any calls came in. Now we had time to kick some fireman butt in cribbage. We offered a wager that the losers had to cook breakfast for the winners, being way overconfident. The firemen were smart enough to know that was a losing proposition for them no matter who won. I found out later that Sammy was a pretty good cook, though. The firemen were great guys who took good care of Sammy and me.

The first call that came was from Bob. Hannah was going to be deported. He was making arrangements to put her on a flight that very evening. She was being sent to Switzerland and he assured us that he would give us the flight information as soon as he made her reservations. Jaden had not appeared at her hearing. It reminded me to call Krissy and Luis to find out what they had heard. Luis said Jaden was back. He had seen him at the Rainbow on Sunday night. Jaden told him he was not going to return to the house. He figured I would have it under surveillance, so he was staying with one of his mobster friends until he found out what was going to happen to Hannah. Luis said Jaden was bristling with rage as he talked about how I was harming Hannah, and it made Luis afraid to ask Jaden for any more information. "He said that once he figured things out he would go back to the house to move out all of his important things. He was pissed at the contractor for not killing you by now. I got the feeling the contractor had split with Jaden's money."

Just before lunch, we received a message that Tony had returned my call. His secretary put me through to him as soon as I returned his call. He answered the phone by asking, "What is this all about?" He didn't sound upset, just anxious. I told him that something had come up in a murder investigation that involved him, something that was critical for him to know. Even though he pressed me to tell him more I refused, saying it was a matter we could only discuss face to face. He relented and said he could meet with us the next evening. He told us to be at the desk in the lobby of his building at 8pm sharp. He would have someone there waiting for us.

This was such a big hurdle that it even surprised Billy when we called to give him the news. All of us were anticipating that Tony would refuse to meet with us. Then Bob called back to tell us that Hannah was booked on a red eye flight out of LAX. He gave us the boarding information, "Just in case you want to wave goodbye." We agreed that it wouldn't be nice to have her leave without a final farewell. More importantly, maybe we would catch Jaden doing the same thing. That would be sweet.

We timed our arrival at the airport a few minutes before boarding time. We walked to the boarding area for Swissair. From a distance we could see a small group of people standing with Hannah, saying their goodbyes. We remained about 25 yards away. Some of the folks in her party noticed us. Our attention was diverted to scoping the area for Jaden, but he was nowhere in sight. We turned our attention to Hannah just as she turned toward us. I don't know who she was expecting to see, but we barely had time to wave before she passed out, flat on the floor, splat! Airline personnel called for medical assistance while her friends bent over her. Each of them found time to look up and glare at us as if we had done something wrong.

Hannah recovered and was ushered aboard her flight in a wheel chair. Sammy and I were approached by a woman from Hannah's party. She identified herself as Hannah's mother. She came ready for a fight. She was dressed in expensive clothes, an attractive middle-aged woman. She demanded to know why we had come to harass her daughter at a moment of great sorrow for them. "Which one of you is Duke?" she demanded to know. I started to point at Sammy, but he knew what I was up to and gave me the look. I confessed it was I, and she verbally attacked, "Hannah told me you have been telling everyone dirty things about her and me."

"Ma'am, I didn't even know Hannah had a mother, but now I can see where she got her beauty," I calmly replied. She took a moment to reassess the situation and took a deep breath. "I have not been happy with Hannah. She has been educated in the finest schools, travelled Europe and can speak several languages. She is very bright and yet chooses low-lifes to associate with. She's been a mess since she's been with Jaden."

"Maybe Hannah getting away from him will be a good thing."

"He wouldn't come here. He knows I can't stand him and the gentleman over there is my husband. He's a federal court judge and Jaden is afraid of him. Jaden treats Hannah like trash. I believe he's a violent man. I've always wondered how he got all of the money it takes for his life style. Hannah said he's staying here to take care of some business deals. I know they were married, so there's not much I can say. Hannah's dad is an ambassador. She's going to stay in his home. He will spoil her, and will overlook anything that he doesn't like. His reputation, you know. I had been asking her to move in with me, but not with her drugs or friends. She seemed really frightened about something tonight; do you know what that could be?"

"We plan to arrest Jaden for murder when we find him. He killed someone that Hannah knew, and she may be afraid of being dragged into the case because of Jaden," I answered, "you are very perceptive to recognize that he is dangerous. Do you know what kind of drugs she was using?"

"She told me that Jaden got her addicted to heroin, but that she could quit whenever she set her mind to it."

Hannah's mother shook our hands and thanked us for talking to her. On the drive home, we came up with an excellent idea. Since we would have about a six hour drive to San Diego and back, we would sleep in tomorrow, and I would pick Sammy up at noon.

Before I left the next morning, I called Bob to tell him about our trip to LAX. I was curious as to how he would track Hannah's movements. "The attendants on the plane told us that she made a scene upon boarding. She was wheeled to a seat in the back of the plane where she started cussing at the attendants. She demanded to be seated in first class and produced $400 in cash to upgrade. She threatened everyone with the fact that her father's an ambassador and was waiting for her in Geneva. "They let her ride in first class rather than make a commotion." Bob explained that they would continue to track her movements in case she left Switzerland. He assured us that he had a way to do that, and would keep us informed. I thanked him, and promised him lunch at Barragan's later in the week. Then I called Dave, and promised him the same. I also updated him on the events at the airport, but I was careful not to say anything to anyone about our trip to see Tony.

Billy had cautioned us not to say a word to anyone. "Too many people don't know how to keep their mouth shut, and Tony has contacts everywhere. You must remember to show him respect. I am amazed that he agreed to meet you guys. You didn't threaten to hurt him, did you? Because then I might get a call to lean on you boys, and you wouldn't like that."

Sammy told him we wouldn't try to fight him because we could both outrun him. Billy laughed and said, "You wouldn't be the first guys to make that mistake."

• • • • •

Our assignment allowed us to travel anywhere our work took us. We had the freedom to do that without informing anyone, even though we always kept our commanders informed out of our respect for them. We left for San Diego that afternoon without informing anyone.

XVII. *GODFATHER*

Before destruction the heart of man is haughty. But humility goes before honor. (Proverbs 18:12)

When I arrived at Sammy's house, we spent some time going through some of the material we had compiled in two accordion folders on this case. We removed Jaden's mug shot and wrote his name and address on the back. I stuck it in my shirt pocket. We had dressed in sport coats and slacks for the trip, although we didn't wear ties.

Riding with Sammy was an education for me. I loved listening to him talk about the cases he had worked and the situations he had been caught up in, some funny, some dangerous. I'm sure he never realized how much I learned from him as we discussed how we would handle various situations. He would have laughed at the idea of teaching me anything, because he never made it seem like he was teaching. We would never disrespect one another that way. Truth is, we worked so well together that we never had to be concerned about what the other would do, especially in interviews and interrogations. We both believed in using silence as a tool and we never interrupted one another. It was almost uncanny how we always seemed on the same page. We didn't talk about how we were going to approach Tony, we just knew it would happen and it would be interesting.

We arrived early, even though our inferiors who ran the country had reduced the speed limit to 55, as if that would fix the gas shortage. We walked around the area until eight and then entered Tony's office building. Waiting in the lobby were two men in suits. They were obvious muscle who looked as if their ties were choking them. We normally would have something funny to say, but we were going to pay heed to Billy's advice and show respect to everyone, even these fellows. They escorted us to the lobby elevators and rode to the top floor with us. The elevator opened to a fine dining restaurant. We were ushered to a table and the body guards asked what we would like to drink. We asked for coffee, and one of the men left to get it while the other stood guard over us. Before we finished the coffee, the maitre'de came over and whispered to one of our escorts. We were told that as soon as we finished our coffee, Tony was ready to see us.

We were escorted back to the elevator where one of the men took out a key and used it to unlock the floor just below the restaurant. The elevator stopped at the unmarked, private floor. We exited and crossed the hall into a large office, led by our escorts.

The office was rectangular, with rows of high back chairs on the long sides, facing across the room to other chairs. There was room for a conference table between the chairs, but there was no table this evening. At the end of the room was a large wooden desk with a smallish, elderly man seated behind it. He probably appeared smaller than he was because of the size of the desk. He had his hands folded under his chin and welcomed us as we entered. He motioned for us to sit on the chairs to his right. Our escorts took seats on the opposite side. There were three other men in suits already seated across from us, and the body guards sat next to them.

It was just like being on the set of The Godfather. There were large portraits on the walls and behind Tony was a painting of a pope. The room was lighted by chandeliers.

Tony was cautious but friendly, and started things by introducing the men across from us. Two were his attorneys; the third was his son who also was an attorney. He then said he had no idea how his name could have come up in anything to do with crime. He told us of his family's influence in the business community, and that he was a good Catholic who gave much to charity. After his opening monologue, he gave us permission to speak.

I told him how much we appreciated him taking time out of his important schedule to meet with us, and assured him that the meeting would be beneficial to him. The touchy part involved getting rid of his attorneys. I told him that our information was very personal, and we would be unable to tell him in the presence of witnesses.

We expected resistance, but to our surprise, he simply dismissed everyone else from the room. They exited without a word, and we were alone with the godfather, although we figured he had the room bugged.

I then took the time to relate how Jaden had become a suspect in our murder investigation. I embellished the story a bit, "He is a heroin addict who does a lot of business from Tijuana to Los Angeles to the east coast. He tells everyone that he is a made man in the mafia and that he works directly for you. He has identified you as the godfather on the west coast. He has a contract out on my life and has made an attempt to kidnap my fourteen year old daughter."

Tony was politely taking this all in without changing his demeanor. When I stopped, he sat in silence for a moment. Then he responded in a way we could have scripted, "I have no idea who this character is. You must know by my reputation that I am a legitimate businessman with no connections to any crime organization. Besides, I don't do business in Los Angeles."

It was hard to keep a straight face as he played the role of a legitimate business man. Sammy had checked earlier with the federal agents who work our bank team at RHD and they confirmed the organized crime connection of Tony and his family. Tony had just been released from federal prison. He must have crossed paths with two of his brothers who were on their way to the joint for tax evasion. Sammy and I managed to stay serious and respectful as we calmly listened to Tony repeat himself, saying, "I've never heard of this fellow Jaden and I don't do business in Los Angeles. If you want, I can make some calls up there tomorrow just to see if anyone I know might be able to help you."

I told him that we believed him, and asked if he could understand why it was so important for us to give him this information. "If anything happens to me, you'll become involved in the investigation just because of Jaden saying he works for you. It

140

would be embarrassing to your family at the least, and possibly damaging depending how the press reports it."

He insisted that he would like to help us but could not, and stood to signal the end of the meeting. As we approached him to shake hands, he whispered to me, "You wouldn't happen to have a picture of this Jaden fellow would you?"

I reached into my shirt pocket and pulled out the mug shot I had prepared for him. I laid it on his desk upside down, so he would see the address. Sammy and I thanked him again, and he expressed his feelings over the danger we were facing. The body guards were waiting in the hallway and escorted us from the building.

We laughed a lot on the drive home, talking about how these things play out when both sides know the other side is acting. "Is it life imitating art, or the other way around?" I asked as Sammy drove.

We wondered what would happen next. Sammy said he would check with Billy the next day in case he hears something. After Sammy drove himself home, I took the car and sped home with the windows down, and the radio turned high.

It seemed as if I had just fallen asleep when the Metro officers woke me up. "You're getting calls from RHD," they informed me. I looked at the alarm and it was an ugly sight, 7am. The troops told me the captain had left a message for me to call as soon as possible. Before I could make the call, the phone rang. Assuming it to be the captain, I was surprised when the caller identified himself as an attorney, one of the horny lawyers, Peter. He said he had an emergency message for me that could only be delivered in person, and asked me to come to his offices on Sunset Boulevard immediately.

I called the captain. He was upset, which was rare for him. He asked what we had been doing in San Diego. This caught me by surprise. I told him it was a routine interview that we arranged regarding Max's murder. He calmed down, telling me he had been awakened by the chief that morning, "It seems that the guy you interviewed was under federal surveillance. They were being helped by San Diego PD's intelligence unit and the two of you were identified. The chief was then contacted, and questioned about his officers meeting with a mafia boss." I remained silent and the captain said to come to the office after meeting with Peter.

I woke Sammy up to tell him I was on my way to pick him up. He said it would be a good thing if we suited up for the day. I hated that.

XVIII. _PLEASANTON_

It was now over a week since the contract on my life was placed. Sammy and I were wondering if the threat was over. It was an atrocious time of morning to be driving to the Sunset strip, and the traffic was already clogged. We would not be very amicable by the time we arrived at the law office. It was located in a professional building near the center of the strip. The lobby door was open and the register showed that the penthouse was Peter's. The elevator doors opened into his waiting room where he was waiting.

He seemed taken aback at seeing Sammy and said he wanted to talk to me in private. I refused, but he said he could not give me his information unless I was alone with him. To my regret, I let a sleazy lawyer come between me and my partner. I would later feel like crap, knowing that Sammy was one of the best friends I would ever have and someone who would always watch my back.

Sammy took a seat in the waiting room. Peter led me through a glass door onto the roof of the building. We stood outside, and he started telling me all of the things I had done to upset important people and how difficult it was going to be for him to keep them from making charges against me. He became redundant with the threats, telling me there would be civil suits from Hannah's family; an internal affairs probe; and possible civil rights charges brought by Hannah's step-father. When he seemed to be running out of threats he said that Hannah's father wanted to use the power of government to seek a federal investigation into my behavior. When he could see I wasn't bothered by any of this, he pulled out his ace in the hole, "And worse than anything else, you have angered people in organized crime who could do harm to you or your family."

I had enough of his bullshit, and told him so. I walked inside, telling Sammy that Peter had nothing of significance to say, and had wasted our time. Peter hadn't asked me any questions. It was clear that he was just trying to occupy my time, but I didn't know why and I didn't feel threatened by this creep from the horny lawyers club.

I tried to apologize to Sammy. He just dismissed it as if it didn't bother him, but I could tell it did. We tried to figure out why Peter had involved himself in our case at this time, and in this way.

•••••

We headed for Parker Center as we continued our discussion. We knew Peter was a mob attorney. We knew he had represented Hannah at her deportation hearing. He was involved in our case and trying to mess with us, but we still couldn't figure out why.

It turned out that the captain was not concerned about our visit to see Tony. He said he had determined that the San Diego PD intelligence captain had made the call to our Organized Crime and Intelligence Division. His officers had located us upstairs, and then saw Tony's escorts lead us away. They had reported their observations to the captain of our OCID who then reported it to the chief. "Whatever you guys do, it seems like the chief always gets the call before I do," he smiled, "I wish you could do it the other way around."

He said he had ironed things out with the chief and it was forgotten, but he wanted us to bring him up to date on what we were doing. We told him and the lieutenant about the visit to see Tony but left out the part about giving him a mug shot of Jaden.

We had lunch at Barragan's, then headed back to West Hollywood. Jaden's place in the hills still looked vacant. We worked our way around to the back in an attempt to see inside. It was a lot easier during daylight. The sliding door on the patio was unlocked, so we let ourselves inside. The furniture was there, but the closets had been emptied. Clothing had been left tossed around in the bedrooms, as if someone had packed in a hurry.

On our drive back to the valley, we received a radio call that Bob had tried to reach us from his INS office. We drove to the fire station and called him. He wanted to inform us that after Hannah landed in Switzerland, she took a flight to Rome, and that she is still there. We decided that we had time to follow up on George's request to meet with us and called Dave at DEA to work out the details. He told us he was free the next day and could meet us in Pleasanton. We decided to go home as the next day would be a long one with a lot of driving. It would be too far to drive both ways in one day, so we would stay overnight in the bay area. That meant submitting documents for travel so we could draw per diem money for the trip. We had to turn around and drive back downtown, but that made suiting up worthwhile. We could make all of our appearances in one day. We put in the necessary paper work and it was approved. We then had to walk it over to city hall to get our funds.

Sammy and I had wives who did not work, so we never had any extra money. It was a mystery to us how some of the detectives we worked with seemed to have big homes and drive big cars and always have cash in their pockets. We never figured it out.

• • • • •

After mapping out the trip, we called Dave back to see if we could move our meeting back a day. The Pleasanton prison was located in Dublin, just east of San Francisco. We figured it would be better to have a driving day, stay overnight and visit George the following morning. Dave said he would adjust his schedule to fit our plans.

Our drive north was pleasant and allowed us several hours to get to know one another better. I told Sammy how my dad had been addicted to gambling, and how I tried to follow in his footsteps. He talked about his parents, also. His dad was Hungarian and his mom was Italian. His dad had a strong work ethic but was a harsh man at home, contrary to my dad who was just absent at home.

Sammy was very good at calculating gambling odds. He knew the casino games and was well aware that you can't beat the house, but he loved playing craps and blackjack. He told me he had gambling blood in him, and he enjoyed trips to Vegas to test his skills. We found a nice motel, had a good meal and called Dave's office to let him know where we were staying. Then we crashed for the night.

The next morning we received a call from Dave telling us where to meet him for breakfast. As we ate, Dave gave us the instructions for visiting George. Pleasanton was recently opened, and was part of a new politically correct operation by the Bureau of Prisons. He warned us that we were not allowed to call it a prison. "It is a correctional institution, and the people serving time are not referred to as prisoners or inmates. They are residents." We had a good laugh, but agreed to abide by the rules so we wouldn't put Dave on the spot. Otherwise, we would have enjoyed messing with the system. So would Dave.

We arrived at the prison and were admitted through the gates. There were lockers where we checked our weapons, then Dave gave us a mini-tour. There were two large buildings, attractive and landscaped inside the prison fence. A lake was between the buildings. Dave explained that part of the new thinking was to experiment with housing both men and women at the same institution. They were separated by the lake. We asked him how it was working out. "There's already a number of pregnancies, and a male resident was found floating in the lake last week. They don't know if he was murdered, or just drowned trying to get a piece of ass."

We followed directions to George's cell, actually referred to as his residence. George invited us in to look around. It was his own private apartment, with divided rooms, nice furniture and a television in his living room. "Pretty nice digs," George said as he had us take a chair in his living room. "I've been staying in touch with all of my sources to see what I could find out about Jaden and the guy who took the contract on you. The motive for Jaden bumping off Max was because he was getting too big and moving in on Jaden's business. Since Max's murder, Jaden's business has boomed. He's on top of the heroin traffic and does not want to lose that, not even if it means having you killed. He was infuriated that you had Hannah deported. He came back to L.A. to see her. He got to visit her using some forged identification with another name. Since Hannah left the country, I can't find anyone who has seen Jaden." He turned to Dave and asked, "Have you checked with INS to see if Jaden left the country?" Dave told us that he had checked with Bob that morning and there is no record of Jaden leaving on any flights, "at least under his real name."

George had really good connections, and most of his information was current. Yet, he was unable to find out anything about the guy who took the money from Jaden to kill me, other than a possible name of Rand. "No one seems to know who the guy is or where he came from and no one has seen him around," George said as he apologized for not getting more information. "I'll keep trying and let Dave know if I get anything new."

We told Dave and George that we had visited The Ball after hearing that Rand likes to hang out there. I had called my cousin, a robbery detective for Santa Monica P.D. He told me where The Ball was located, and arranged for one of his detectives to meet us there. It is a members-only club, so he would get us in and show us around. When we arrived, we discovered that my cousin hadn't told me everything. It was a nude club.

We gained entry with the help of the detective, and the three of us went to the bar for drinks. As we sat at the bar, a naked woman came up and put her arm around the Santa Monica detective. After they kissed, he introduced her to us as his fiancée. Wow, did that raise some questions for Sammy and me. She stood there in her birthday suit while we described what we knew about Rand. She said she'd talk to all of the girls, and if she got any leads she would pass them on to her sweetie. These were helpful folks, but we couldn't even imagine how a marriage like that could last without somebody getting killed. When I told my cousin about it, he said it wasn't a secret to his department. We could have never pulled that off at L.A.P.D.

We had time to kill, and spent it talking to George about his legitimate interests in business. Then we asked him what the scoop was on the guy who was found floating in the lake. He said, "That is a funny story. Everybody knows the guy drowned by accident. A couple of the inmates saw it, but they weren't going to stick around and get busted.

"The guy who drowned was from south central. He'd never been in water outside of his bathtub, and even that wasn't frequent. He just got so horny that he thought it would be easy to swim. The joke is that his johnson was so big it acted as an anchor, and pulled him under. If he was smart, he would have tied a sail to it and gone across on his back."

Dave took us to eat in the commissary with some of the guards. It was a nice, open air facility, and the food was good. "Not your daddy's kind of prison," one of the guards said. We asked about the drowning in the lake. One of the guards told us the people in charge, government wonks, the ones who created the problem, were now the same ones responsible to correct it. They decided the best thing to do was to drain the lake. "How will they separate the men from the women?" we asked. The guard answered, "They are going to hold sensitivity classes. They actually believe more knowledge is going to get these people to change their behavior." Everyone shook their heads in disbelief. I silently had a conversation with the Lord, "This guard just summarized one of the themes of your word, that desire always trumps knowledge. I wish I could find a church that provides one-on-one help for people who want to sort out the issues of their hearts."

I was getting angry. It always calmed me to remember that God has not changed his purpose of doing love, even though he continues to allow himself to be victimized as people ignore and mock him and his word. "I don't know how you tolerate it, Lord, but if you do, so can I. I know on the day you make justice your purpose, people will know that you are the Lord."

"Justice is coming," I said aloud and everyone gave me a puzzled look. I just smiled and finished eating.

• • • • •

Back at the motel, Sammy and I had the same idea. Since everything seemed to have calmed down, and we were so close to Nevada with the city money in our pockets, why not take a short cut home through Tahoe. We didn't have to think long about that. We threw our clothes together and took off. We made it to the north shore in about an hour.

I hadn't been to Tahoe before, Sammy had. He was driving and pulled into a casino. I had been listening to his logic about shooting craps, and taking the odds on the numbers. It made sense to me, so I changed all of the money I had into chips and headed for the crap table. Sammy told me he was going to try his strategy on blackjack.

The casino wasn't very crowded. I rolled the dice a few times, just staying even. A crowd started to come in, and all of a sudden I started rolling numbers. I was winning all of my odds bets, but Sammy hadn't told me the strategy behind taking money off the table while on a hot streak. I kept letting it ride and making passes. A crowd started to gather wanting to get in on the action. I had so much money on the table that a guy next to me told me to start taking it off. He said I had well over a thousand dollars on the table. I told him I would quit after one more roll, since I had all of the numbers covered. Predictably, I rolled a seven. I walked away with nothing, and never knew how much money I had left on the table. It didn't matter now, because I was broke.

When I found Sammy, he was sitting at a blackjack table playing his last ten dollars. He lost and asked me if I had any money. We hadn't gotten permission to take a city vehicle out of the state, and now we were broke, low on gas, and sort of like illegal aliens. Sammy tried to cash a check, but was turned down. I had no checks, and no money in my checking account anyway. We talked about people we might call to send us money to get home. The only person I could think of was my dad, but I figured he wouldn't have anything to send and would be upset at me for not being a better gambler.

My dad was a hard working man. In the 1950's I saw him bring home weekly pay checks of over one thousand dollars. Yet, he gambled it away. After my mom had died, I wondered what it was like for her to try to run the house and buy groceries without money. I also knew that she would get phone calls from people who told her that my dad owed them money. Poor mom. She really loved dad but was afraid to tell him what it was like being married to him.

Sammy got an idea. He talked to one of the dealers who told us to drive to the south shore and try to cash a check. He gave Sammy the name of a casino that he was sure would do it just because we were police. It wasn't a far drive, but we were really low on gas and hadn't eaten for a while. Sammy had nothing. I checked my pockets and found a dime. We bought a donut and split it in half.

We had been given a good tip. The casino cashed Sammy's check, but now he was worried at what he was going to tell his wife about taking the budget money out of their bank account. Then he had a great idea to eliminate the problem, "Why don't we take the money and win back what we've lost?" We agreed to stay away from the dice and to hit the blackjack table. I said, "At least I know how to take my money off the table in that game, and my dad taught me how to play cards."

So we did it. We walked by all of the dealers, picking an attractive female dealer at an empty table. We were both dressed in levis, but there was something about the look that tipped people off as to who we were. We started with small bets, amazed at how she continually dealt herself over 21. We kept increasing our bets, and she continued to bust. We were raking in our winnings when the pit boss came over and removed her. Someone in the camera room must have gotten suspicious. We had won back half of the city money, so we decided to hang out for a while to see if the dealer came back on the floor. We dropped some small change in the slots for about 30 minutes and then we saw the lady coming back.

It was crazy. We sat down at her table, and starting winning every hand, even the hands where we doubled down. We won over twice what we had lost at the other casino. Then they came and took the dealer away again. Funny how good life seemed all of a sudden. We each gave the lady fifty dollars, and then bought ourselves steak dinners. We were pretty puffed up as we headed back to Los Angeles. We drove all night and slept in the next morning.

• • • • •

Things had quieted down with Hannah gone and Jaden nowhere to be found. Sammy and I started going over the files of a triple murder that I had been working on before Max's murder. The victims were from Baltimore, and I had spent some time on the east coast gathering information. Sammy got caught up in the case, and thought we had enough to file it with the district attorney. We started working out a strategy on working the Balto case, but kept checking with the usual suspects to see if anyone had heard anymore about Jaden.

I showed Sammy the autopsy photos of Charles Smith, and asked him what he thought. He said, "This guy almost looks like you, except he looks better dead than you look alive."

We finally received a call from Bob at INS. "Hannah has left Rome. She took a flight to Amsterdam. We don't know what she's up to."

XIX. _AMSTERDAM_

Their feet run to evil and they hasten to shed blood. But they lie in wait for their own blood, they ambush their own lives. So are the ways of everyone who gains by violence, it takes away the life of its possessors. (Proverbs 1:16, 18-19)

Hannah was sitting at one of the wooden tables inside the Hofje van Wijs enjoying a cup of hot tea. She was familiar with this place, once known as the tea and coffee suppliers and purveyor to the queen. It had been established for hundreds of years. From her seat she could see the canal outside the window. She was watching for Jaden to arrive.

Inside, she watched a party of little girls enjoying high tea. Hannah looked away. She was feeling particularly alive this day and didn't want anything to trouble her. She looked great, dressed in a bright red blouse to accent her flowing blonde hair. She wore a red ribbon in her hair.

Seeing Jaden approach caused her to have second thoughts about being seen with him. It had been over two weeks since she arranged a room for him here in the heart of the red light district. Her friends from Rome, Guisepte and Donatella, had offered to share their small apartment with him until she could come. She had stopped using narcotics since she had seen Jaden, and was already feeling healthy. Jaden was shuffling his way along the sidewalk looking seedy and shabby. She knew what would make him feel better.

He came through the door and smiled when he saw her. She stood and embraced him. "Do you have something for me?" he asked. Even though narcotics were legal here, she knew he was broke. "Right here," she said, patting her purse. He took her hand and said, "My room is right around the corner, I need to go right away."

Hannah picked up her things and they headed for the door. She noticed one of the girls from the tea party was watching her. The blonde haired, blue eyed Dutch girl smiled and waved. She almost felt like crying, remembering how good it felt to be innocent and free. She had a flashback to happy times as a child when her parents were together, and she knew she was desired for who she was rather than for what her flesh offered. She allowed herself only a passing thought that she quickly shut down, bringing her back to her current reality.

The room was on Oudezijds Achterburgwal. It was an old building that faced the canal. The first floor had once been occupied by a business, but that was in better days. Today it sat vacant, nothing more than a giant trash receptacle. They walked down an alley to the stairs leading to the second floor of the blighted building. When they arrived at room #12, Jaden led the way inside and closed the door. They embraced again. He had tried to clean up but his breath was bad.

When Hannah determined no one else was there, she asked, "Where's your bedroom? I've got a surprise for you." He led her to a small room with a bed and a night stand. He had already laid out his heroin kit on the table. "You are so beautiful you take my breath away, I've missed you," he told her as he stepped out of the way so she could lie on the bed.

She took him by the shoulders, and turned him so his back was toward the bed and said, "You first, I've learned some things since we left the states." Jaden lay back on the bed, and Hannah stuffed a pillow under his head. He was proud of his woman. He watched her remove a small foil from her purse and open it. In all the years they had been together she had never given him a fix, yet it was something he always wanted. He could hardly believe it was finally happening, and he was ready to lay back and enjoy the moment. He was already anticipating the pleasure that was on the way.

He closed his eyes as Hannah put the heroin in a spoon and held a lighter under it to cook it into a liquid. Then she took Jaden's syringe and drew the liquid into it, using a cotton ball as a filter. Jaden felt her tying off his upper arm, and looked to see that she had taken the red ribbon from her hair for the purpose of raising the vein. She gently pushed the needle into his vein until she saw a bit of liquid appear, then she slid the needle all the way in and registered it, drawing back a little on the syringe. When she saw blood appear, she knew the needle was in the vein.

At that point, Jaden laid his head back on the pillow and closed his eyes. The effect of the heroin was immediate. Jaden had never experienced such a rush. He let out a sigh, "Baby, like a thousand orgasms, I'm on my way to heaven."

Jaden was transported away to place where he could feel nothing but pleasure. He enjoyed the feeling without moving, he was paralyzed by the rush. Within a few minutes, Jaden was feeling so good that he was not aware he had stopped breathing. Even if he knew, it wouldn't have mattered to him. He slowly rolled his head toward Hannah and opened his eyes. She wasn't there. He looked down and saw the syringe hanging from the vein in his arm. His only thought was that the red ribbon was gone. He smiled and closed his eyes, never to open them again.

● ● ● ● ●

Hannah was back at Hofje van Wijs. She had ordered her favorite tea on the menu, Darjeeling Second Flush. When the waiter brought the tea, she took it to the pay phone and placed a collect, long distance call. The man who accepted the call sounded sleepy, and she quickly computed the time difference. It was 3am in Del Mar. "I have a message for the boss," she said. "Please have him call me from a secure phone. I'll wait where I am." With that she gave him the number of the pay phone. She knew the man who answered. He was called Frankie because of his penchant for singing Sinatra songs. She had no idea what his real name was, but knew it was his job to screen calls for Tony. She expected his response, "This better be real important. Even if it is, you may not hear from anybody 'til morning."

She sipped on her tea and waited. In about twenty minutes the pay phone rang. She knew it would be from a secure line used by the mob in Del Mar. When she answered, she said, "It's over." There was a pause, and then Tony asked, "Has he been found yet?"

"No. His roommates aren't due for a couple of hours, it's still daylight here. I'll be watching for them to come home, and call the police. I'll just walk in and act like a good wife should. Before I go, can you tell me how you knew he was going to be in Amsterdam when you told me to get a room for him?"

"Sure, I had Peter keep the homicide detectives busy while my boys rousted Jaden out of bed and put him on a private plane. I knew when he was going, and I knew where he was going. He had no choice."

"He didn't suffer, did he? I gave him the dose that I got from your friend here in Amsterdam."

"Hannah. Jaden was a fool who would have eventually taken all of us down. It was the drugs. You, of all people, know what that means. At first, he got mouthy with my boys. I gave them permission to rough him up for all of the crap he put me through. As far as the fix you gave him, he went out just the way he would have wanted. It was over 25% pure, the best he'd ever had. Tony chuckled, "You know, those detectives who came to see me had some kinda balls. I enjoyed the way they played along with me, leaving a mug shot of Jaden on my desk and all. They knew I would have to do something to protect myself. I actually respect those guys. Where will you go after this is over?"

Hannah paused for a moment, and said, "I think I'll go back to Rome. You don't think I'll have any problem getting the insurance money, do you?"

"I told you it's good, I've checked on it already. You're going to be a wealthy girl, as rich you are beautiful."

Hannah hung up wondering if Sammy and I would ever know that she was the one who tipped the feds when Jaden put the contract on my life.

It was a couple of weeks later that we received a letter from the Amsterdam police informing us of the death of Jaden. Their report told us that a woman named Hannah had come from Rome to visit her husband. She cried when they told her he had overdosed, but said she wasn't surprised. She supplied a marriage license, and claimed the body. It was their understanding that she had the body cremated.

Officially, their coroner had ruled it an accidental death from a heroin overdose, a common cause of death in the neighborhood where he died. Hannah had confirmed that he was a heroin addict, and that she had traveled to Amsterdam to try to convince him to stop using.

The report read that she had given the police my business card and told them Jaden was wanted for murder in Los Angeles.

●●●●●

The captain had kept the Metro officers at my house, even though things seemed to have cooled off. He didn't want to make a mistake. On the day the Amsterdam letter arrived, he and the lieutenant went to Barragan's with us. Then Sammy and I took off early. I picked up my family at Larry and Shirley's and we went home together.

After we expressed our heartfelt thanks to the Metro officers, including hugs from the kids, they left out the front door. I followed them out. Officer Biting turned to me and said, "Duke, I forgot to tell you something. This morning we received a call from the homicide lieutenant at Rampart Detectives. He said to tell you that his men gave up on the Charles Smith murder, saying no one would ever solve it. He said he sent it to RHD with a note to the captain to assign it to the only guys who might figure it out. What's up with that?"

I smiled and said, "That's another story."

XX. _DEBRIEFING_

Watch over your heart with all diligence, for from it flow the springs of life. (Proverbs 4:23)

I last saw Rose in 2003. She was living in the same small house where she had raised Max. She was bedridden and had lost a lot of weight. I was passing through Joliet on the way to a business meeting in St. Louis, so I only had a few minutes. I didn't tell her I was coming; I just walked into her bedroom with permission from her caretaker. She was speechless when she saw me. It took a moment for her to react, as if she wanted to make sure she wasn't dreaming. She wept and held me for the entire visit. She had been asking me for almost 30 years to write the story about the murder of her son. Before I left, she told me that for all these years, she had regretted not taking my offer to move to California and live with my family.

When I started writing The First Crime Scene in January of 2008, I called to give her the news. I knew how happy she would be and that she probably wasn't going to believe me. I called daily starting on January 11th. There was never an answer and she didn't have a machine to take a message. On January 18th, her caretaker answered the phone. I identified myself and asked for Rose. She said, "Rose died on January 11th.

• • • • •

After our captain retired, he moved from Los Angeles. I didn't communicate with him for many years before hearing about his death. He called once to let me know that Art had been placed in a convalescent home.

• • • • •

Our lieutenant retired and left Los Angeles, moving to be near his children. He and his wife enjoyed many years before his wife died. Shortly thereafter, he started suffering from dementia that led to Alzheimer's. His den contains a wall map of the Pacific Islands. As a Navy Corpsman in WWII, he was present at the landings of our troops on each of the islands. The last time I saw him he no longer remembered who I was or the many significant things that he had accomplished in his life. He had attended church with me a number of times, bringing his father.

• • • • •

Art was a gifted athlete, a clown and a character that everyone loved. After his retirement we continued to play golf together. One year, we won the Police Celebrity Golf Tournament, playing with Lawrence Welk. Welk invited him to appear on his television show. Art was an excellent ballroom dancer, and was featured on the show dancing with his wife. When I was told that Art was in a convalescent home, not expected to live, Sammy and I visited him. What we didn't know was that his wife was also in a wheelchair. We brought them together, and watched them pretend they were dancing in their wheelchairs. Both died shortly thereafter.

• • • • •

Billy and his wife became dear friends after I retired. They both gave their lives to Christ, Billy calling him, "The Boss." I had the privilege of renewing their wedding vows and officiating at their funeral services when they passed. Billy went first from emphysema, his wife a few years later from cancer.

• • • • •

Sammy is retired. After we worked together at RHD for over five years, he was promoted and placed at the head of a multi-agency narcotics task force that was charged with investigating major drug rings infiltrating southern California from south of the border. He was the best policeman I ever met in my law enforcement career. We still dream of telling all of the stories that the Lord let us live through, because each one was a unique adventure that most detectives never experience. At the end of our career at RHD we were told by Chief Gates' adjutant that an audit of RHD records revealed that Sammy and I had solved more homicides than the rest of the division combined.

We now get to give our grandchildren something precious that our children suffered without: our time and attention.

3921072

Made in the USA